THE JOURNEY

A SEARCH FOR THE ROLE OF CONTEMPORARY ART
IN RELIGIOUS AND SPIRITUAL LIFE

Usher Gallery in ~~association with Redcliffe Press~~ *Lincoln*

Lincolnshire County Council Recreational Services

Front cover – South Transept, Lincoln Cathedral.
Back cover – *Glen Onwin*, Subterranean Fire, 1984.
Frontispiece – *John Piper*, Lincoln Cathedral, 1961. Collection Usher Gallery.

Project Co-ordinator: *Judith A Robinson*
Design: *Richard Devereux*
Typesetting: *A·C·T·S* of Lincoln. Set in Bembo
Colour Reproduction: *Graphics + 4* of Hull
Printing: *Rayprint* of Lincoln

Dimensions in cms; height precedes width

Published by the Usher Gallery in association with Redcliffe Press Limited,
with the financial support of the Dean and Chapter of Lincoln, the Henry Moore
Foundation and Lincolnshire & Humberside Arts.

ISBN 0 948265 99 X

Acknowledgements

Albemarle Gallery · Christer Salen · The City Arts Centre, Edinburgh · The Dean and Chapter of
Lincoln · English Heritage · Fabian Carlsson Gallery · The Henry Moore Foundation · The Henry
Moore Sculpture Trust · Heritage Lincolnshire · Lincoln Cathedral Preservation Council · Lincoln
Cathedral Clerk of Works Department · Lincoln Minster Arts Trust · Lincoln Theological College ·
Lincolnshire and Humberside Arts · North Kesteven District Council · Rev Canon John Bayley and the
Parochial Church Council of the Church of St Mary Magdalene with St Paul-in-the-Bail, Lincoln · Rev
G S Richardson and the Parochial Church Council of the Church of St Mary, Stow · West Lindsey
District Council.

CONTENTS

Preface

THIS PUBLICATION takes its title from a major visual arts project on the role of contemporary art in religious and spiritual life, organised by the Usher Gallery, Lincoln, in the summer of 1990. Situated below the Cathedral in Temple Gardens, the Usher Gallery houses an extensive collection of topographical paintings, prints and drawings of the Cathedral and religious buildings throughout the County.

In recent years, many galleries have felt the need to reach out into the wider community, creating opportunities for artist and public to meet and for the exhibition of contemporary art in non-gallery locations.

A number of such outreach projects have been initiated by the Usher Gallery, of which *The Journey* is the most complex and ambitious to date.

From 17 June until 12 August, a series of unique site-specific installations of contemporary art is being created in a group of religious and secular buildings, and public spaces in the City and Diocese of Lincoln. A documentary and contextual exhibition is being held at the Usher Gallery, accompanied by the New Icons exhibition of new Christian art, curated by Rupert Martin, and an appropriate selection of topographical works from the permanent collection.

An extensive programme of educational events is also being arranged, including artists-in-residence, workshops, guided tours, lectures and a conference on the place of the contemporary artist within the life of the Church.

The complementary and independent publication introduces the work of the fourteen artists participating in the project and develops themes and issues raised in a series of commissioned essays by artists, writers, critics and representatives of the Church.

The Journey arises at a time of widespread discussion of the relationship of contemporary art and the spiritual. It is hoped that the project will contribute to this important debate and act as a focus for the particular opportunities and areas of work that it represents.

The project has been achieved as a result of successful collaboration between many organisations and individuals, to whom the Usher Gallery is most grateful.

I would particularly like to thank the artists for their enthusiasm and commitment in the making and lending of their work, and the authors of the essays for their contributions to this publication.

I would also like to express my thanks to Garry Fabian Miller for his inspiration and partnership in the initiation and organisation of *The Journey*; Canon Rex Davis and Canon Dr. John Nurser for their vital co-operation and support; and to Robert Hopper for his support and commitment at a crucial stage in the development of the project. Special thanks are also due to Jo Brogden, Roger Bryan, Richard Devereux, Dr. Peter Hayes, Canon Bill Jacob, Heather Lees, Mick O'Connor, Roger Parsons, Jean Pritchard, Rev. John Pryor, Clive Redshaw and John Sansom for their invaluable advice and assistance.

We are greatly indebted to our sponsors and thanks are particularly owed to the Dean and Chaper of Lincoln, The Henry Moore Foundation, The Henry Moore Sculpture Trust and Lincolnshire and Humberside Arts.

The Journey aspired to create an opportunity for renewed dialogue between the artist and the Church and for a new engagement between gallery and community.

I hope that the achievement of the project will be measured, not only by the final results but also by the experiences shared and the lessons learned by all concerned along the way.

Judith Robinson
Assistant Keeper of Art
Usher Gallery, Lincoln
April 1990

The Journey

Garry Fabian Miller

ALONE IN THE GREEN ROOFED CAVE, alone with the sunlight and the pure water, there was a sense of something more than these. The water was much more to me than water, and the sun than sun. The gleaming rays on the water in my palm held me for a moment, the touch of the water gave me something from itself. A moment and the gleam was gone, the water flowing away, but I had them. Beside the physical water and physical light I had received from them their beauty; they had communicated to me this silent mystery'. Richard Jefferies.

We experience moments of transformation at rare intervals in our lives. Fleeting and unexpected they are often accompanied by an expansion of perception, a heightened sense of what has been, what may follow and more particularly our relationship to a greater whole. Artists, writers, musicians, poets often speak of the attempt to relate the specific to the universal, the fusing of the spiritual with the physical, perhaps feeling more keenly than most the pulse of creation. For those with faith, art becomes a celebration of God's radiance, a gift, received then shared. For those of us less confident, arrested for a moment from the frenetic spaces we daily inhabit, a work of art may unexpectedly sing to us. Giving ourselves up to its emanation, wondering at its beauty, recognising its emotional nourishment we shun any association with God, though some of us might admit to a vague notion of the Spirit. Faced with this flow of energy from an inanimate object and often deeply moved, we are puzzled.

Buildings acquire an ambience from their use. The unadorned space of a Quaker meeting house, deeply silent, is conducive to contemplation and meditation, to prayer. The great Cathedrals charged with the accumulation of acts of faith, through successive generations, provide sanctuary, tranquility, clear water within the turbulent stream of our existence. Their architecture, slender ascending pillars interweaving in the vaults overhead, soaring spaces seeming to reach to heaven were meant to be uplifting and remain so today. When we pray we become still, quiet, giving of ourselves. When we look at art we somehow seek to allow its aura to work upon us, slowing down the pace of our perception to accommodate the resonances of our surroundings. The capacity of art to inspire reverence, assist devotion and thus instil faith has long been recognised by the Christian Church. The lavish embellishment of the Gothic Cathedrals, often with leaves, flowers and buds celebrates the God given creative energy of nature just as much as stained glass showing biblical stories and the lives of the saints is testimony to the spreading of the Word of God. The longing for art to express a spiritual dimension is nowhere more clearly evident than in the rose window. Its circular, radiant form can be seen as an expression of the human aspiration towards wholeness and coherence. The Figure of Christ, often found at the centre, can be reached by many paths, this corresponding to the many ways which lead to the real self at the centre of the soul.

The Dean's Eye Window, North Transept, Lincoln Cathedral.

This image became the metaphor for 'The Journey'. The unfolding pattern of a life, following many paths in a search for meaning and direction. For some this is understood as a linear path toward enlightenment, for others it is a continuous process, in which the nature of the journey brings fulfilment; there being no point of arrival, only a constant flow.

Each period produces and should commission work which confronts and reflects in its language and iconography, the moral and emotional concerns of its time. Following the Second World War a great surge of art was commissioned for churches which reflected the horror and guilt of the immediate post-war period; a disbelief in man's inhumanity to man, the Prisoners of Conscience. These very potent and often challenging works spoke to many, often becoming important symbols within collective worship and individual prayer.

Since this particular body of work, it is difficult to see other areas in which the spiritual needs of the individual and the community have brought forward a new period of support and inspired the commissioning of contemporary art.

This may be changing. For a number of years there has been an increasing awareness of both the fate of the earth, and the joy and hope contained within nature. Slowly our minds, for so long channelled into areas of control and dominance over the earth, are beginning to open. Our confused and misguided thinking shielded a great sense of fear and inability to accept our place within natural cycles.

Friends Meeting House, Brant Broughton, Lincolnshire.

A concern for nature has resulted in some of the richest and most beautiful work found in our churches and cathedrals; evident to in their architecture and sculpture.

This tradition continues to inspire many new forms and ideas within which many of the artists in *The Journey* are part. Their work reaches toward this, and with that of others, we hope will form a new body of work which will enhance the fabric of religious and secular life as we edge towards a new century.

The Journey has been a remarkable project to be involved with; marked throughout by mutual sharing, respect and responsibility. I hope that as people experience the works, whether through participation in church services, alone in silent prayer and reflection, or by chance as a tourist, that their perceptions of art and faith will be challenged.

I hope that the encounter will result in a reaffirmation of each and effect a positive commitment to, and belief in, the spiritual values which give meaning and purpose to our life and acts. From this, perhaps, will flow a new cycle of commissioning of contemporary works that will fill our religious buildings with confidence.

Dartmoor
Spring 1990

Vine, Capital 11,
Chapter House, Southwell Minster

The Journey as Pilgrimage

Rupert Martin

THE IDEA OF *THE JOURNEY* contradicts the notion of art and its exhibition being a static enterprise confined to museums. While works of art may have been commissioned for houses, civic buildings or churches, many end up in the context of a museum, isolated from their original setting and a context in which they can be better understood. Furthermore, by its method of display, a museum can unwittingly encourage a superficial way of looking, whereby we spend only a few seconds with each picture, and tend to see them on the move, although museums are not to blame for an inability to concentrate on pictures or for our visual illiteracy. Despite this, much has been made recently of the idea that museums have supplanted churches as the places for spiritual nourishment, and the new museums springing up in Europe, America and Japan, are often called the cathedrals of our age. In his essay printed in the *New Statesman*, *Art in a godless society*, Waldemar Januszcak writes about the way in which such museums set out to create a 'phoney religiosity', and invest art objects with a sanctity verging on idolatry: "Today's modern masterpiece hangs on its pristine white gallery wall like a precious altarpiece. Instead of communion rail it will often have a rope stretched between elegant supports in front of it to keep the congregation on their side of the spiritual divide. If it is a piece of sculpture it will stand in splendid isolation in the centre of the room, like a font or baldacchino, communicating nothing so much as its own sanctity and spiritual presence." [1]

Despite its inevitable limitations, the museum can still provide us with memorable experiences of works of art, enhanced by the use of the new technologies in conservation and restoration. In recent years, however, following the precedents of Brancusi and Henry Moore, attempts have been made to create or display works in other contexts, such as the home – Les Chambres d'amis, Ghent; the city, Münster – the park – Kergúehennec, Brittany, and the Yorkshire Sculpture Park; the forest – Grizedale and the Forest of Dean; the Country House garden – Powys Castle; and the converted cloth mill; Dean Clough, Halifax. Conspicuous by its absence, however, is the setting of church or cathedral. Despite the post-war rebuilding for which much new work was commissioned, the visual

[1] Waldemar Januszczak, "Art in a godless society", *The New Statesman*, 14 August, 1987, p.22.

Magdalena Jetelovà, *Place*, Oak, 1985–6, The Forest of Dean.

arts have only occasionally animated these spaces, usually owing to the initiative of individuals such as Walter Hussey. This is partly because of the complex and costly nature of commissioning new works of art, and partly to the difficulty of integrating art objects into churches already cluttered with objects and memorials. The freedom to explore and experiment in *The Journey* is due to its temporary nature. The other aspect of the project which sets it apart from previous isolated endeavours is the way in which a number of disparate elements are being brought together in a variety of places to provide a complex set of relationships within a city which has for long been a centre of pilgrimage.

The title, *The Journey*, has a pleasing lack of religiosity about it, and the sub-title – *A search for the role of contemporary art in religious and spiritual life* – suggests the idea of exploration and discovery. It also points to the concept of pilgrimage as a valid one when considering visiting a place in which works of art have been embedded like jewels in a reliquary. Not that there is any superstitious veneration of relics or dusty bones, but rather a dynamic creativity being expressed within the context of places that are resonant with history and spirituality, Lincoln Cathedral and Castle, the Old Bishop's Palace, the Rest and several Churches and Chapels. A visit to *The Journey*, a journey in itself, could well be undertaken in the spirit of a pilgrimage, testing and enquiring, searching and finding. Each work of art in its particular

Henry Moore, *Upright Motive No. 1*, Bronze, 1955–6, known as the *Glenkiln Cross*, situated on the Keswick Estate, Dumfriesshire. Resembling a celtic cross, "a kind of worn-down body and cross merged into one", as Henry Moore called it, the sculpture is superbly located on the brow of a hill in Scotland.

location could provide a story on which to meditate, a 'Lincoln Tale', both enjoyable and devotional. The three aspects of a pilgrimage – the path, the place and the object – are unified by the challenge of encountering works of art in unexpected but appropriate settings, and participation might develop an awareness of how the sacred and the secular can converge within a particular space.

The Path Itself

There is a sense in which the journey is in itself sufficient. Bruce Chatwin wrote in *The Songlines*; "When Karl Barth came to account for the dearth of ritual among the Basseri – or of *any* rooted belief – he concluded that the Journey itself was the ritual, that the road to summer uplands was the Way, and that the pitching and dismantling of tents were prayers more meaningful than any in the mosque." [2] The journey becomes an end in itself, not just a means to an end or a way of achieving some tangible goal. The sestet of one of Rilke's *Sonnets to Orpheus* encapsulates this idea:

only when some pure Whither
outweighs boyish insistence
on the achieved machine

will he who has journeyed thither
be, in that fading distance,
all that his flight has been. [3]

The contentment and inner peace that comes from walking along the simple path with no anxiety about the destination or the future is often expressed by those who should have most to fear from the future. Father Anatoly Shurakovski is able to write from the prison at Sosnovets in the USSR in May 1934, five years before his death: "I am here doing general duties.... How good it is to know that everything lies in God's hand, that there is no special work to be done for him and no special place to serve him in, that any work and any place is right. Like this narrow stony path which winds its way through miserable pine trees and bushes which are only now beginning to come into leaf: it is his path. Or the work with trees and planks which we haul out of the wood; it is his work, I am serving him. And even these wooded huts with their slatted beds, they too can be his mysterious kingdom full of grace." [4]

The idea of the path, the way or the pilgrimage is also connected to that of ascent. The act of walking humbly with God, of following his path is one of spiritual ascent, an ascent that does not exclude the physical world, and which does not necessarily involve greater knowledge, but a deeper penetration into the dark

[2] Bruce Chatwin, *The Songlines*, Jonathan Cape, London, 1987, p.201–2.

[3] Rainer Maria Rilke, *Selected Works*, Vol. 2, Translated by J.B. Leishman, The Hogarth Press, London, 1960, p.264.

[4] *Cry of the Spirit*, Christian Testimonies from the Soviet Union, Selected from the Journal *Nadezhda* by Tatiana Goricheva, Fount, London, 1989, p.128.

'cloud of unknowing'. St John of the Cross writes:

"The farther that I climbed the height
The less I seemed to understand
The cloud so tenebrous and grand
That there illuminates the night. [5]

It is significant for *The Journey* that Lincoln Cathedral, being on a hill, involves us in a physical ascent, and that the sculpture by Keir Smith consists of a series of cloudscapes, carved in stone, and placed in a progression up the gradient of Temple Gardens below the cathedral. It is a timely reminder that the path of discipleship is not without discomfort or pain and that the difficulty of the journey corresponds to the desirability of what we learn along the way. At the end of *The Quaker Graveyard in Nantucket*, Robert Lowell depicts the culmination of a pilgrimage to Walsingham:

"There once the penitents took off their shoes
And then walked barefoot the remaining mile;
And the small trees, a stream and hedgerows file
Slowly along the munching English lane,
Like cows to the old shrine, until you lose
Track of your dragging pain." [6]

The Space Within

Although the journey is in itself sufficient, for most there is also a goal, a place to which they come and an object of interest, a focus of devotion which motivates their journey. The object cannot, however, be separated from the space which it occupies or the place in which it is situated, with all its cultural and historical accretions. Just as the light gives it substance and form, so its location and immediate context give it meaning. An object, whether it is a work of art or an object of devotion or both, can either occupy or create a sacred space, a territory demarcated by architecture, a vessel brimming with light, darkness, sanctity. The sacredness of a space cannot be presumed, but it can be entered into. The prayers which have been said for centuries in a church, chapel or cathedral leave no residue like the waxy smoke of candles on the rafters, but an invisible presence which can be detected by the soul if it is prepared; just as paper will receive an image onto its surface if it has been sensitized to respond to the light. To some extent faith is involved in apprehending God's presence in a place, but sometimes the work of art can act as a catalyst, setting in train a reaction in our hearts. The object may or may

[5] St John of the Cross, *Selected Poems*, Translated by Roy Campbell, Fount, London, 1979, p.33.

[6] Robert Lowell, *Lord Weary's Castle*, Harcourt, Brace and World, New York, 1974, p.19.

not be invested with a transparent beauty, but it can become a vehicle for emotions which otherwise could not be articulated. Robert Lowell's poem continues:

> "Our Lady, too small for her canopy,
> Sits near the altar. There's no comeliness
> At all or charm in that expressionless
> Face with its heavy eyelids. As before
> This face, for centuries a memory,
> *Non est species, neque decor,*
> Expressionless, expresses God." [7]

The sculpture, statue, picture or icon are all objects to which emotions unique to the beholder can be attached. Their meaning cannot be pinned down and they interact not only with the space which they occupy, but also with the individual who approaches them for whatever reason.

The works in *The Journey* have a particular appropriateness to their setting but are not limited by it. Richard Devereux's *The Bowl of Grain*, situated in the Morning Chapel of Lincoln Cathedral, suggests the dawn of time. Placed on an oak altar is a fragment of stone with the incised words "BEYOND THE SOJOURN, man returns, beckoned by the outstretched hand, sharing the destiny of a single grain". Referring to the birth of agriculture and of civilisation, a single grain of wheat is placed on the altar, symbolising the idea of death and rebirth which we find in John's gospel when Jesus says; "Unless a grain of wheat falls to the ground and dies, it remains only a single seed. But if it dies, it produces many seeds. The man who loves his life will lose it, while the man who hates his life in this world will keep it for eternal life." [8]

The location of works in relation to architecture is a vital part of the project. Stephen Cox's *Rock Cut: Holy Family* placed on a cloister wall, draws its inspiration from the temple carvings of Southern India, and re-interprets the Nativity of Christ in the light of this tradition and in the black, rust-stained granite of India's ancient landscape, as the artist describes it: "Never submerged except as magma thrust up during the creation, its mountains are atomised by millennia of baking wind, the source of India's ever-swirling dust. Voluptuous, caressed, the shapes of landscape mirror its sculpture." [9] Cox's fusion of Christian iconography with the forms of Indian carving is part of a number of contrasts which his sculpture sets up. The raw surface of the fragments of rock arranged in a spiral, contrast with the refinement of the relief carving of the three figures, set in a cave-like recess. In the elegant architecture of a gothic cloister, the work may look incongruous, but its inclusion

[7] Ibid. p.19.

[8] St John's Gospel Chap. 12:24–25.

[9] *Stephen Cox,* The Tate Gallery, London, 1986, p.21.

Stephen Cox, *Holy Family*, Pen and Ink, 1986. A drawing which relates closely to figures in *Rock-Cut: Holy Family*, Granite, 1986.

points to the universality of Christ and his origins outside Western culture in the Middle East. A more purely formal juxtaposition is achieved in the placing of Richard Long's Slate Circle in the South Transept beneath the Rose Window, setting up resonances of pattern, material and light which challenge the viewer to see afresh the connection between the spiritual and the material. Garry Fabian Miller's work set in the small, intimate space of a chapel embodies the idea of light emerging from darkness. In a cluster of three photograms, layers of reed and grasses exclude the light except in the middle where it is filtered through a single yellow reed to suggest light breaking through like a candle flame in the darkness. Miller's works are conducive to prayer and contemplation, and take us from the tiny interior world of grass and reed to the idea of the separation of light from darkness embodied in the act of creation itself.

In the Cathedral, in which the four works described above are located, the space also changes from the intimate to the immense, from dark to light, from chapel to soaring nave. The movement of the columns and tracery upwards and outwards, contrasts with the inward, enclosing shells of each chapel. The cathedral disrupts our conventional notions of scale and contains within its architecture the movement of the soul in worship between prayer and praise. A Cathedral also provides a pilgrimage within a pilgrimage, as one moves from chapel to chapel, from nave to transept enacting a journey within. The works of art seem small in relation to the Gothic vaults, and yet, paradoxically, by focusing our gaze, they transport us in imagination beyond the finite limits of stone and glass into an infinite yet intimate space.

The Return

The point of a pilgrimage is not just to return with souvenirs like the badges which pilgrims bought in the Middle Ages. What you come to see must be left behind, but you can also leave something of yourself behind, and return enriched by new insights, a different person. As T.S. Eliot writes in *Little Gidding*:

> "We shall not cease from exploration
> And the end of all our exploring
> Will be to arrive where we started
> And know the place for the first time." [10]

Above: The Tattooed Cross from *J. Sanderson, Travels,* 1584–1602. Many pilgrims, while rejecting pilgrim badges, were ready to be tattooed as a sign of a completed pilgrimage.

[10] T.S. Eliot, *Collected Poems,* 1909–62, Faber & Faber, London, 1974 p.22.

We take something intangible away with us on the return journey which can illuminate our everyday lives. Perhaps it is the understanding that the sacred and the secular, the path and the place, the object and its enveloping space cannot be separated, that the sacred inhabits the ordinary, that the Incarnation is not a myth and that it is possible for God to enter our world in human form, just as his spirit gives life to our bodies. By its nature a search or exploration, *The Journey* attempts to dissolve some of the artificial boundaries and barriers we put up, and by bringing together past and present, by integrating works of art into works of architecture, shows how contemporary art can exist within and animate historical or religious places and in doing so re-awaken our interest in the close relationship between art and faith.

The Journey

ARTISTS

Roger Ackling

Craigie Aitchison

Stephen Cox

Richard Devereux

Jennifer Durrant

Garry Fabian Miller

Jon Groom

Sue Hilder

Eileen Lawrence

Richard Long

Leonard McComb

Glen Onwin

Peter Randall-Page

Keir Smith

Stephen Cox LINCOLN CATHEDRAL

The Mediterranean is the womb of my civilisation, a limestone basin whose crustacea have accumulated and been thrust up to form mountains, vivacious, containing marble metamorphosed by compression: light, translucent, young enough to have memories to yield up.

The high places of Dravidia, says Forster, have faced the sun for longer than any other place on earth with 'forms that were his before our globe was torn from his bosom' *(A Passage to India)*. Never submerged except as magma thrust up during the creation, its mountains atomised by millennia of baking wind, the source of India's ever swirling dust. Voluptuous, caressed, the shapes of landscape mirror its sculpture.

Man has defined his gods in this land where the closeness of the earth's crust lends little mystery to his origins, black hole or polished black granite. The navel of the cosmos realised in meditation. *Om* its first sound, light exposing form, the sculptor fashioning it. The gods live within the sculpture, within the stone where the answer has always lain regardless of its identity, Ganesh, Brahma, Siva, Vishnu, the hen that laid the 'Cosmic Egg' that floated in the Primal Waters. [1]

[1] Stephen Cox, Tate Gallery, London, 1986.

Stephen Cox,
Mahabalipuram 1985

Rock Cut, Holy Family by Stephen Cox, to be installed on the west wall of the Cloisters of Lincoln Cathedral.

It seems appropriate that Cox has gone back to a representation of creation and the physical origins of perception, by means of working in an ancient stone which has never been overlaid by sedimentation and which still dominates the structure of an ancient land.

The most significant part of that situation in which Cox created these works is the place itself, Mahabalipuram, a small town fifty kilometres from Madras that lies low on the coastal plain. The ground is sandy and from it rise several granite outcrops: a hill and huge rocks. Some of these have been carved into four small temples, the Rathas, archetypes of sacred design twelve hundred years ago, an elephant and a cow. The flank of the hill, a vast rounded boulder some fifty metres long is encrusted with figures in relief; gods, spirits, people, animals. Several portico temples are cut into the granite face of the hill, their back walls carved in over-life size relief. Another temple, built on rocks jutting out into the sea, is defended by a wall of caves. The style of all this sculpture of the seventh and eighth centuries is, compared with much other Indian art, informal, fresh, even a little ingenuous. The subjects, though theological, are realised rather as everyday life. A European is reminded of the vitality of the late middle ages and early Renaissance that were to come six hundred years later. But there is nothing in western sculpture that has this quality and yet is so grand, above all nothing that is integrated in the same way into the matrix of nature. […]

The figures of 'Rock Cut Holy Family' seem closer in type to the Hindu triad of Siva, Parvati and Skanda with their rather opulent physique. The raised fingers however suggest the heaven-pointing gesture of christian art. The substrate of granite fragments on which it is carved, though literally autochthonous, is disposed in a way that seems very western. It suggests the technique of building by setting one stone on another with its implied eventual ruination by dispersal rather than the Indian technique of carving out with its implied dissolution by erosion. Cox's own creative technique had involved fracture and dispersal. The Tamil process of powdering individual crystals that he was now using resembles erosion and part of the subject of the sculpture is that Indian technique. Represented on the separated stones is apparently the basic motif of a cell that is cut into the rock and the relief that is revealed on the back wall, a relief that could never be broken in the way that a relatively shallow applied relief could. The relief 'quoted' in this work is fuller than in other large scale works by Cox. In this rather subtle way the formal means as well as the nature of the representation express a fundamental difference between the traditions, even when they seem to be dealing with a closely related theme the sacred family as an expression of diversity in unity. At the same time they cross over and are themselves an expression of that same diversity in unity. [1]

[1] 'The Art of Stephen Cox', Michael Compton. *Stephen Cox*, Tate Gallery, London, 1986.

[24]

Stephen Cox
Rock Cut: Holy Family, 1986.
Granite 274 × 426 × 15
Courtesy Christer Salen.

Between open palms the ears of corn
relinquish their swollen grain.
Offered, when light and dark
balance for the second day.
The ascending act beckons the knowing hand
to open the doors of stone.
Within the chambers' enfolding gaze
fall seeds to meet the earth once more;
the intervening breath binding
man to rock and grain.

Richard Devereux
1989

Richard Devereux has made a new piece, *The Bowl of Grain*, for
installation in the Chapel of St Mary Magdalene, or Morning Chapel
in Lincoln Cathedral.

BEYOND THE SOJOURN

*man returns, beckoned by the outstretched hand
sharing the destiny of a single grain*

Richard Devereux
The Bowl of Grain (detail), 1989-90.
Stone fragment – Hoptonwood stone, enamel and gold leaf.
43.2 × 67.5 × 3.2

... the discovery of agriculture radically changed the conception of human existence: it proved to be as frail and ephemeral as the life of plants. Yet, on the other hand man shared the cyclical destiny of vegetation [...] since man's life is like the life of cereals [grain], strength and perenniality become accessible *through death*. The dead return to the bosom of Mother Earth, with the hope of sharing the destiny of sown seed; but they are also mystically associated with the stone blocks of the burial chambers and consequently become as strong and indestructible as rock. [1]

Chun Quoit, burial chamber (SW/402340), West Penwith. c. 3,200–2,500 BC.

[1] Reprinted with permission from *A History of Religious Ideas, Vol. 1* by Mircea Eliade © 1978 by The University of Chicago; All Rights Reserved.
Originally published in French under the title *Histoire des Croyances et des Idées Religieuses, Vol. 1*: De l'age de la pierre aux mystères d'Eleusis © Payot, Paris, 1976.

[2] *Indications from Signs*, Abd al-Kadir as-Sufi. IQRA 1979.

[3] *The Chinese Written Character as a Medium of Poetry*, Ernest Fenollosa. New Directions.

[4] *The Word as Intellectual Image. The sculpture of Richard Devereux*. James Cowan – (Extract from unpublished essay).

In Arabic, 'kalimat', meaning 'words', is derived from a root indicating speech, importance, authority, ascendancy and its core meaning 'to wound, cut or slash'. [2] It is therefore important to note the incisive, blade-like nature of words as an instrument of expression. We cannot do without words, indeed without language, since it is by their use that truth is expressed. Whereas in nature the expression of truth may be registered as a flash of lightning, for men the very act of speaking the truth is a *transference of power*. [3] Thus Devereux is appealing to a primal instinct in us when he asks us to enter into the profoundly hieraticized field of force that surrounds his word sculptures. At once he is endeavouring to reach out to us with all the vividness of what we see, as well as with the mobility of the sounds that we hear. [4]

I consider myself priviledged to have two of my paintings placed in the magnificent and awe-inspiring cathedral at Lincoln.

In his essay, David Miller delineates most perceptively, those areas of interest/speculation, which I believe my paintings may address – namely "The intangible [...] a paradoxical stillness of seemingly floating forms [...] The overall effect of immateriality and 'inwardness' ". [...]

"The process of discovery occurs through an artistic or painterly exploration, in which shapes, colours, lines, textures are subject to various combinations and transformations; but each ensemble of combinations and transformations has a resonance, a significance, in relation to that image-field; so that in the act of artistic exploration there lies hidden (so to speak) an exploration of certain aspects of existence." [1]

The cry for wholeness in our lives is our attempt to find a way home. At its most eloquent it can be heard in the sophisticated prayers and mantra of the seasoned disciple, but failing this one can employ the most simple prayer in the universe, namely the cry for help. To cry out for help and then be willing to accept whatever follows is often the only way of picking ourselves off the ground and continuing our journey. [2] [...]

Carl Jung, who spent much of his working life researching the phenomenon of the acceptance of our shadow, summed up the vulnerability and emotion surrounding acceptance by saying: "That I feed the beggar, that I forgive an insult, that I love my enemy in the name of Christ, – all these things are undoubtedly great virtues, what I do unto the least of my brethren I do unto Christ. But what if I should discover that the least among them all, the poorest of all beggars, the most impudent of all offenders, yea, the very fiend himself – that these are within one and that I myself stand in the need of the alms of my own kindness, that I myself am the enemy who must be loved – what then?"

"We are all planetary citizens, whether we know it or not." [...]

"We are all passengers in time and space, and the trip will be joyous or disastrous depending on how we behave towards each other." [3]

The earlier Quietists regarded the soul as something that came from the outside to dwell in the body. But to the Taoists, Tao was something that was at the same time within and without; for in Tao, all opposites are blended, all contrasts harmonized. [4]

[1] *Jennifer Durrant and the Poetics of Painting,* David Miller, Serpentine Gallery, 1987.

[2] *The Dance of Change, An Eco-Spiritual approach to Transformation,* Michael Lindfield.

[3] Sally Swing Shelley, Chief U.N. Education Information Programme.

[4] *The Way and its Power, The Tao Te Ching and its place in Chinese Thought,* Arthur Waley.

Jennifer Durrant has made two new paintings inspired by a visit to
Lincoln Cathedral, to be sited below the East Windows of the
North and South Aisles.

... Sacred hoop of my people was one of many hoops that made one circle, wide as daylight and as starlight and in the centre grew one mighty flowering tree to shelter all the children of one mother and father. And I saw that it was holy.[5]

Images, Yeats says, are living souls. The seat of the soul is where the inner world and the outer world meet, where they overlap, it is in every point of the overlap.

My paintings are not the conscious re-creation of an exterior space; they are perhaps concerning my internal space. My thoughts and imaginings are prompted by those particular and quite distinct things that I observe in the outside world and by my identification with them and my feelings toward what I see. [...]

I believe paintings are themselves, they have their own completeness, but that completeness is not only about staying there in front of the painting; I really do think that a painting is actually taking you off to some place else of your own imagining.

I do think that a painting may be rather like a mandala, in the sense that its use may be of a meditative or contemplative sort.[6]

Art is not thought or emotion, but expression, always expression. To keep an idea living intact, tinged with all its original feeling, its original mood, preserving in it all the ecstasy which attended its birth, to keep it so all the way from the brain to the hand and transfer it on paper to a living thing, with colour, odour, sound, life all in it, that is what art means, that is the greatest of all the gifts of the gods, and that is the voyage perilous.

On her tombstone:–

That is happiness; to be dissolved into something complete and great.[7]

Jennifer Durrant
May 1990

[5] Black Elk. American Indian.

[6] Jennifer Durrant, *The Experience of Painting*, South Bank Centre and the Laing Art Gallery, Newcastle, 1989.

[7] *Writings of Willa Cather,* 1873 – 1947. Journalist, editor and fiction writer. Found in a small local museum on Grand Manan Island, New Brunswick, Canada.

Jennifer Durrant
We are all Passengers, 1990.
Acrylic on canvas
265.4 × 318.8

Garry Fabian Miller LINCOLN CATHEDRAL

When her doctor took her bandages off and led her into the garden, the girl who was no longer blind saw 'the tree with the lights in it.' It was for this tree I searched through the peach orchards of summer, in the forests of fall and down winter and spring for years. Then one day I 'was walking along Tinker Creek thinking of nothing at all and I saw the tree with the lights in it. I saw the backyard cedar where the mourning doves roost charged and transfigured, each cell buzzing with flame. I stood on the grass with the lights in it, grass that was wholly fire, utterly focused and utterly dreamed. It was less like seeing than like being for the first time seen, knocked breathless by a powerful glance. The flood of fire abated, but I'm still spending the power. Gradually the lights went out in the cedar, the colors died, the cells unflamed and disappeared. I was still ringing. I had been my whole life a bell, and never knew it until at that moment I was lifted and struck. I have since only very rarely seen the tree with the lights in it. The vision comes and goes, mostly goes, but I live for it, for the moment when the mountains open and a new light roars in spate through the crack, and the mountains slam. [1]

[1] 'Pilgrim at Tinker Creek', Annie Dillard, Picador 1975.

Garry Fabian Miller has made a new group of photographs for the
Longland Chantry, a quiet chapel of prayer and meditation
in Lincoln Cathedral.

"Garry Fabian Miller's art is essentially concerned with looking, with taking the time to see in truth and to respond in honesty: in other words, it is about contemplation. [...] Light is not a symbol, for Miller, any more than it was for Jesus. A symbol is by definition a finite thing. It 'stands for' something else. But light is only radiantly itself, active and alive. Just in being it draws us into some contact with the infinity of the Creator."

"Miller makes no secret of the fact that his art is a spiritual activity. It is a form of prayer, and equally, paradoxically, a form of proclamation. It is as much passive as active, as is all true prayer, and both elements are of importance. He creates from his own experience, looking at nature from the depths of a personal life that is his alone. He gives nature time to unfold within him, to make sense of him of his own human confusions, to give hope to him in his own human longings, to complete within him his human inadequacies. The immediacy of all this is made so much more profound by Miller's technique. He does not take away with him merely a memory of what he has seen and experienced amidst woods and gardens (often his own garden). But he physically carries away the actual leaves from which his insights came. He is their camera, bypassing the distance of the mechanical process. Immediacy is a keyword in Miller's work, his own immediacy leading hopefully to ours. We who see what he has created are drawn into the profundities of his experience, mediated now by our own different personalities but equally compelling."

"Critics speak about the haunting beauty of what Miller does, but there is in truth little one can say about his art. Words cannot convey the effects of actually seeing, which means 'contemplating', the transmitted light, (as opposed to reflected light) shining through leaves in their pure reality. Stains of acid rain, the tears of time, the wounds of insects, all are held up before us with love and reverent attention. The wounds are as much part of nature's beauty as are the perfections. One can philosophise about all this, or about Miller's own commitment to ecological movements, but intellectualising misses the point. It is each one in the heart's privacy who has to 'consider', to 'lift up your eyes and see'; no one can do it for us. Perhaps in this incommunicable aspect Garry Fabian Miller is at his most contemplative. He shares with us his vision so as to awaken our own. Like the light, he is a medium, a way of reaching the goal towards which we all most deeply aspire." [1]

Opposite page
Garry Fabian Miller
January 7, 1990
Light, leaf, cibachrome 35 x 35

[1] Extracts from, *"Garry Fabian Miller – Contemplative Artist"* by Sister Wendy Beckett.

Jon Groom LINCOLN CATHEDRAL

The geometry is the vehicle that carries the message, its simplicity and directness embrace another value; getting beyond the physical to reach a higher plane. Architecture, is like this; it evokes certain states of mind. The proportion, the way a space is divided affects the way we are, and directly influences our temperaments. The building, brick upon brick, becomes something more than its construction, something much greater.

My paintings relate to architecture, they hang on walls, so the placement within a room becomes specific. The interior elements of the paintings are in communion within the surrounding space. The sources and materials used to make art, belong to everyone, there's nothing exclusive about them. It's just a transformation through need, into something else. It's to do with making the ordinary extraordinary.

Jon Groom,
January 1990

Jon Groom
'*Fuse* # 4 1990'
Oil and Alkyd on
zinc and wood
56 × 80.2

Jon Groom has made a new piece in five parts in Lincoln, inspired by
the great East Window of Lincoln Cathedral and to be installed
within the arcading below.

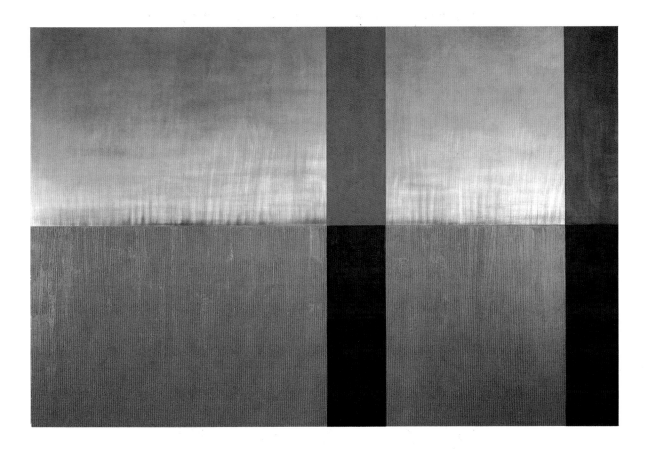

Jon Groom
Evidence # 1, 1989-90.
Oil and graphite on resin and zinc on wood.
101.6 × 152.4

Richard Long LINCOLN CATHEDRAL

The source of my work is nature. I use it with respect and freedom. I use materials, ideas, movement and time to express a whole view of my art in the world. I hope to make images and ideas which resonate in the imagination, which mark the earth and the mind. [...]

I like the idea of using the land without possessing it.

A walk marks time with an accumulation of footsteps. It defines the form of the land. Walking the roads and paths is to trace a portrait of the country. I have become interested in using a walk to express original ideas about the land, art, and walking itself.

A walk is also the means of discovering places in which to make sculpture in 'remote' areas, places of nature, places of great power and contemplation. These works are made of the place, they are a re-arrangement of it and in time will be re-absorbed by it. I hope to make work for the land, not against it.

I like the idea that art can be made anywhere, perhaps seen by few people, or not recognised as art when they do. I think that is a great freedom won for art and for the viewer. [...]

Time passes, a place remains. A walk moves through life, it is physical but afterwards invisible. A sculpture is still, a stopping place, visible.

The freedom to use precisely all degrees of visibility and permanence is important in my work. Art can be a step or a stone.

A sculpture, a map, a text, a photograph; all the forms of my work are equal and complimentary. The knowledge of my actions, in whatever form, is the art. My art is the essence of my experience, not a representation of it.

My inside and outside sculptures are made in the same spirit. The urban and rural worlds are mutually dependant, and they both have equal significance in my work.

My work has become a simple metaphor of life. A figure walking down his road, making his mark. It is an affirmation of my human scale and senses: how far I walk, what stones I pick up, my particular experiences. Nature has more effect on me than I on it. I am content with the vocabulary of universal and common means; walking, placing, stones, sticks, water, circles, lines, days, nights, roads. [1]

[1] *Words After The Fact, Richard Long, 1982* Touchstones, Arnolfini, Bristol 1983.

Richard Long
Sahara Circle, 1987.
Photograph
61 × 85.7.
Courtesy Anthony d'Offay Gallery.

Richard Long
Halifax Circle, 1989.
Cornish slate
6.42 m
Courtesy Anthony d'Offay Gallery.
Installation at Henry Moore Sculpture Trust Studio,
Dean Clough, Halifax, October – December 1989.

Halifax Circle by Richard Long to be installed in the Great South
Transept below The Bishop's Eye rose window
in Lincoln Cathedral.

'ENERGY IS ETERNAL DELIGHT'

WILLIAM BLAKE

A single pebble thrown into a still pond – from the centre – the delight of the vibrations.

Nature is full of unbelievable surprises – the fingerprint.

Light is the thread of Art.

In art it is easy to be personal; the real problem is to speak to strangers.

It is the vision that matters and not the ideas.

The slow building of the watercolour is comparable to adding clay to the armature.

Powerful tension, created through dabs of coloured water.

The space cannot be separated from the beauty of the forms.

Drawing is the architecture of the spirit.

In spring is much movement, in winter stillness – art contains many opposites.

The impossibility to create a painting with a heartbeat – a lifetime is not enough time.

It is easy to begin a painting; to finish a painting is difficult – the difficulty increases.

The beauty of the late Cézannes – the top of the mountain is as a candle flame lighting the plane around.

Leonard McComb, London 1979

First published by the Coracle Press Gallery, London 1979, in the folder of prints *'Blossoms and Flowers'*.

Portrait of *Young Man Standing* by Leonard McComb to be sited in
the north aisle of the Nave and *The Golden Bowl* to be installed in the
Little South Transept near the Chapel of SS Peter and Paul
in Lincoln Cathedral.

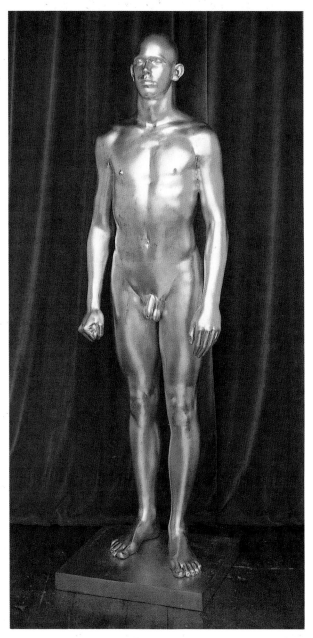

Leonard McComb
Portrait of Young Man Standing, 1963 – 1983.
Polished bronze and gold leaf
175 × 48 × 48

In the winter of 1982–3 Leonard McComb was working with concentration and at considerable length on a new cast, eventually to be gilded, of a life-size sculpture of a nude standing figure. Though he had begun it twenty years before, he still sought, in an already powerful image, an ideal finality of form. Recognisably a work of our own day it spoke eloquently, too, of the art of ancient Egypt. [...]

The creation of a strong identifiable image was inseparable for McComb from the precise realisation of its surface, inch by inch. Thus extended observation of a real model was only the beginning of an equally extended process of refinement, first of plaster and then of bronze, to give maximum articulation to every detail of the structure. By this means the asymmetries within this particular body (and by implication any other) are clarified, even emphasised, while in the hands – one clenched, the other relaxed – McComb's concern with both the outer and the inner life is symbolised by asymmetry of a different kind. As he told Timothy Hyman,[1] against the background of the Cuban missile crisis, the murder of John Kennedy and the Vietnam war McComb created this figure as an affirmation of survival. 'I tried to create an image of a whole person, his physical and spiritual life being inseparably fused [and implying] the embedded capacity for powerful and gentle action, both physical and intellectual'. It is an image of youth, both vulnerable and determined – perhaps unconsciously a self-portrait of McComb in the strangely isolated situation he occupied in the 1960s. But it is also at once a portrait of a particular individual studied by McComb and a symbolic and therefore impersonal image. Its authority has a quality of permanence which while in no way obscuring its date frees it from restriction to the particular era that produced it. [...]

'Art', he has observed, 'is the celebration of God's radiance'. His work witnesses to the rightness of the natural order, seeing all stages in the cycle of life as a unity. At the centre of this vision is his reassertion of human dignity. As Timothy Hyman has written, [2] 'in work after work, McComb has been able to transform and transcend any life-room origins, and to recreate the Body as an act of faith'. [...]

The spirit which is at the heart of McComb's work cannot be separated from his treatment of light, which throughout his art plays a key role, both structural and symbolic. Reflective surfaces or the brilliance of paper can be expected to activate light, but in McComb's work it seems to be generated more dynamically. The sculptures receive and give it out across exteriors refined to a point of formal tension, and the drawings and watercolours through an interweaving of accents which gives the emission of light an active pulse. [...]

McComb's special concern with light is yet further evidence of the visionary nature of his art. It is an art which transforms the detail of the world around us, even as this is celebrated in itself. Each of McComb's works gives an extraordinary

[1] Leonard McComb: Body and Spirit, Timothy Hyman, London Magazine, August – September, 1982.

[2] Ibid.

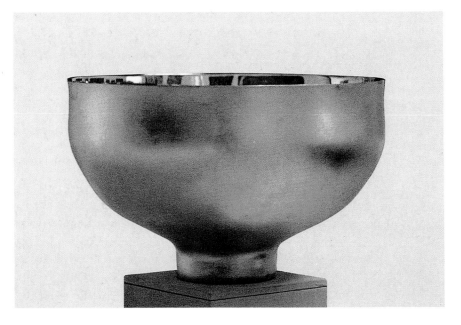

Leonard McComb
Golden Bowl, 1984.
Polished bronze and gold leaf
36 × 57

sense of the actual presence of the motif. But it transposes the motif into McComb's own world of imagination, presenting it with a concentration that gives it a role going beyond the facts of period and place. [...]

The radiance which emanates from every form (as both waves and light) is a manifestation of his conviction of the active interdependence of the two. In insisting on this radiance McComb affirms the principle of permanent renewal inherent in the cycle of nature and of life. Remarkable for its positiveness, his art celebrates this cycle in all its phases and all its parts. [3]

As transcriptions of the perceived world, McComb's drawings and watercolours of figures, still lives, landscapes and seascapes go far beyond surface incident to reveal a heightened structure and substance which is in a sense visionary. In his insistence on the direct experience and knowledge of nature McComb has worked consistently within a longstanding pictorial tradition which in its combination of observation and spirituality is particulary British. [4]

[3] Leonard McComb, Richard Morphet.
Leonard McComb: Drawings, Paintings, Sculpture, Arts Council of Great Britain, London, 1983.

[4] Ibid.
Postword, David Elliott/Joanna Drew.

Eileen Lawrence BISHOP'S PALACE

Celestial
Ascent
Bird of Dawn
Blue
Aureole
Light
Ark

Eileen Lawrence, 1990

Eileen Lawrence *Lincoln Prayer Stick* 67, 1990. Watercolour on paper, 244 x 15

Chapter House, Lincoln Cathedral

Eileen Lawrence has made a series of new prayersticks inspired by a visit to the Chapter House of Lincoln Cathedral to be installed in the upper room of the Alnwick Tower of the Bishop's Palace.

Glen Onwin BISHOP'S PALACE

[1] *Tantric Mysticism of Tibet,* John Blofeld. Dutton, New York, 1970.

Image an illimitable ocean in which there are in-numerable vials. Each vial is filled with sea-water belonging to that very ocean and each is composed of a substance that gradually thickens or dissolves in response to circumstances. Under suitable conditions it dissolves altogether, whereupon the water it contains becomes indistinguishable from the rest of the ocean. Not one drop of water ceases to exist; all that is lost is its apparent separateness. In this analogyj, the water in each vial represents a so-called individual being and the gradually thickening or dissolving vial symbolizes his mental and physical characteristics.[1]

Glen Onwin
Subterranean Water, 1984.
Earth, oil and wax on canvas
mounted on board
213 × 191
Courtesy The City Arts Centre, Edinburgh.

In his essay on Isaac Newton, *'The Secret Life of an Alchemist'* Jan Golinski discusses an important manuscript by Newton of around 1670, now in the Smithsonian Institute, Washington D.C. "In this manuscript, entitled "Of nature's obvious laws and processes in vegetation", Newton distinguished 'vulgar chymistry' from a more sublime interest in the processes of vegetation – in other words, the processes of growth and life, which were thought to occur among metals as well as among plants and animals. 'Nature's actions are either vegetable or purely mechanical', he wrote. Art could imitate nature in either type of operation. The imitation of mechanical changes in nature would be common, or vulgar, chemistry, whereas the art of inducing vegetation was 'a more subtle secret and noble way of working'.

It was that, subtle, secret, and noble way of working that Newton was seeking to master in the course of his intensive chemical investigations." [2]

[2] *"Let Newton Be! A new perspective on his life and works."* Jan Golinski, Oxford University Press.

Firstly the earth floor is coated with hot wax which immediately solidifies and seals the floor, then into indentations in the floor, which are caused by dripping rain water, various solutions of chemicals and extracts from plant matter are poured.

Glass vials containing sea water are placed amongst the solutions. In time the natural processes of organic and inorganic growth, the growth of mould and the formation of crystals, will occur.

Glen Onwin,
March 1990

Glen Onwin is to make a site-specific installation *'Of Nature's Obvious Laws and Processes in Vegetation'*, in the Undercroft of the Bishop's Palace.

Peter Randall-Page BISHOP'S PALACE

Historically niches have been used as a way of integrating sculpture and architecture. My own interest in the device lies in the expressive potential of the relationship between a form and the space which it occupies. This can also be analogous to the relationship between the sculpture and the original block from which it was carved.

The process of carving is the perception of one form contained within another, and in these works I have attempted both to retain a sense of the original block and to allude to the heart of the stone itself. I wanted to evoke a sense of the interior of the stone, drawing attention to a metaphorical as well as a physical inner space.

Peter Randall-Page
April 1990

Peter Randall-Page has made two new carvings to be installed in the
Chapel of the Bishop's Palace.

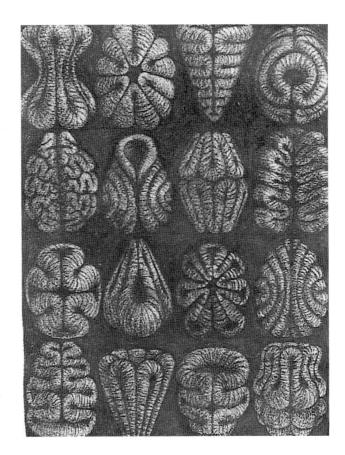

Peter Randall-Page
Sixteen Ways to Keep a Secret, 1989.
Charcoal on paper
76.2 × 55.9

Peter Randall-Page
Ways to Wrap a Stone I, 1990.
Kilkenny Limestone
38 × 56 × 38

JOURNEYS ARE OFTEN A SEARCH
FOR REVELATION. IN THIS TRADITION
SOME OF THE GREATEST HAVE BEEN
MADE BY THOSE KEEPING STILL.

Roger Ackling March 1990

Norfolk	*Colonsay, Inner Hebrides*	*Colonsay, Inner Hebrides*
Summer 1988	April 1987	April 1987
Sunlight on wood, sculpture	Sunlight on wood from shoreline	Sunlight on wood from shoreline
18 × 4 × 2	41 × 9·5 × 2	27·5 × 8·5 × 1

Receding,
falling,
defying
the
outstretched
hand;
bathing
the
wanderer's
soul
which
reaches
upward
to
meet
the
breath
of
unmeasured
time.

Richard Devereux
1989

Two copies of a 'prayer text' were made. One was retained to accompany the stone book, the other was placed in a small recess under one of the standing stones of Long Meg circle in Cumbria. This temporary shelter is part of an ancient temple and in turn part of the silence which predisposes the wanderer to its sacrality.

Richard Devereux *Temple of Solitude (Cast Aside the Time of Men),* 1989. Hoptonwood stone, enamel, English oak and gold leaf 44.5 × 55 × 16.5

The hope within the work is that it should act as a 'mirror' in order to cast light into the differing aspects of *'profane time'* and *'sacred time'.* By crossing the threshold of the ring, both a physical step and a symbolic step are taken. One steps out of de-sacralised time into a time that is completely other. This in turn allows sacred time to intervene, to occur within an instant, without duration. The stranger who stumbles upon the text will take with it a hope; a hope that the words will 'uncover' the significance of a forgotten spirituality, a bedrock of the Divine.

Craigie Aitchison ST MARY MAGDALENE
WITH ST PAUL-IN-THE-BAIL

You have something of a religious background. Your grandfather was a Presbyterian minister for 50 years to the Erskine Kirk in Falkirk. Do you think this has any bearing on why you paint Crucifixions?

No, I don't, but of course it could have.

Have you ever used a model for Christ in the Crucifixions?

No.

Are your Crucifixions always set against the Scottish landscape of your childhood?

It seems they are, but it's not intentional. In fact, there are two recent yellow ones which don't have the hills in them. And the early Crucifixions don't have any hills in them. I put the mountain in when I wanted the figure to be in a special place.

Are the animals that often attend the Crucified Christ meant to comfort or to mourn?

The animals are meant to be upset, concerned. It's as though the animal is walking along and is suddenly amazed and horrified and looks up. But there are Crucifixions I've done where the animal is sitting at the foot of the cross completely resigned.

Why do you leave out so much?

Sometimes I think I don't leave out enough. I don't consciously leave out anything. The Crucifixions always start off anatomically correct with everything in; then later on I might take things out.

Why do you paint a dead bird?

I've had him for 27 years. I found him in Scotland. I never got over seeing him dead on the windowsill in the snow. He was so small. I've painted him since the 1950s, always his exact size; this is the first exhibition he has been in for a long time. [1]

[1] Craigie Aitchison interviewed by Andrew Lambeth. *Craigie Aitchison – Recent Paintings* Albemarle Gallery, London, 1989.

There is no doubt that Aitchison's religious feelings are genuine and profound, though not confined to Christianity. It is probable that he uses its iconography because it has been familiar to him from earliest childhood, and thus with all its associations serves better than anything else as a focus for those feelings; and also, because the imagery is traditional and universally understood, it is a suitable vehicle for communicating them. Seeing so many Gothic and Renaissance religious pictures in Italy where they were done, often still in the very churches for which they were done, made him realise that a whole world of feelings, with which hitherto he had not known how to deal, could be channelled into these subjects, above all that of the Crucifixion. This image, already loaded with associations, ideas, and meanings could be re-charged with his own deepest, most intense emotions, by means of shapes and colours – his natural language for everything – in a way for which no other subject provided the opportunity.

He has always done the figure of Christ from imagination; but, inevitably, his imagination must be furnished with memories, and so, every conceivable pose for this subject having been invented long ago, although his way of painting it is unique, the pose itself must always awaken echoes; and just as, for him, any specific memories may well have been unconscious, so may the echoes be for the spectator; and yet they play their part in the effect, contributing to it the always comforting authority of tradition, however obscurely felt – and sometimes provoking a comparison, a reaction against the new treatment. More than once he has taken out the arms, and even these painfully vertical, hanging figures suggest a memory of the Pergamene Marsyas, which Kenneth Clark connects with Michelangelo's late Crucifixion drawings. [...]

It is a peculiarity of his approach that, while form and colour are of the utmost importance to him, substance is of none whatever. Simplicity and clearness are, however, vital. So these small figures of Christ are unbroken by any marks. Yet they do not have the effect of silhouettes, for they are three-dimensionally conceived, and we feel how the brush made the form, with the slightest possible gradations, working outwards from the central axes of movement, and the dark element in which the figures hang comes up to them, meets and surrounds them, without any contour being drawn. And even though in a few cases the sense of the strained skeleton is more fully realised than usual, we always feel that the figure is of the same substance throughout – that we could pass a sword through it and no blood would flow, it would close up again unharmed, like a flame or a sunbeam, composed of luminous particles cohering, not statically, but in some kind of invisible dance. It is the same with the many small landscapes and still-lives painted during these years; a red rose against a green wall, a small dead bird, a tree and a garden gate, an egg and a milk-bottle, a cup or vase or candlestick, everything has this quality, as if it were the spiritual essence of the thing or person, its very inmost identity, purified from all accidents of the flesh or material body, yet not more substantial than a mirage – an appearance, a reflection, both less and more than reality – suspended in the air.

This certainly contributes to the timeless, non-historical quality of the Crucifixions. They are both symbol and reality, in an eternal present. [1]

[1] An Introduction to the work of Craigie Aitchison, Helen Lessore. *Craigie Aitchison – Recent Paintings* Scottish Arts Council, 1975.

Crucifixion, No 4 by Craigie Aitchison to be installed above the altar in the Church of St Mary Magdalene with St Paul-in-the-Bail, Lincoln.

Craigie Aitchison
Crucifixion IV, 1988.
Oil on canvas
76.2 × 63.5
Courtesy The Albemarle Gallery.

Running from Eden (A River Portrait), 1988

This charts a journey along the Medway, a river I have known since childhood, a journey deep into Kent by rail, following the course of the river, and then by foot towards the upper reaches. The sculpture depicts the river where it is crossed by bridges, where routes intersect. Although this is the most topographical sequence I have attempted the river here, as elsewhere in my work, suggests the passage through life, following the river's course from its youthful upper reaches to the estuary where its identity is lost in an intermingling with the sea. Where the river is seen as finite and living and therefore capable of sustaining an anthropomorphic allusion, I tend to regard the sea as remote, unbounded, unknowable, and consequently alien. It often seems to be a threatening element in my sculpture, a force of nature which obstinately refuses to be tamed, which is capable of great violence and is utterly beautiful.

Keir Smith
March 1990

Running from Eden and *Last Rays of an English Rose* by Keir Smith to be sited round the 13th century font in the Church of St Mary, Stow.

Keir Smith
Caspar's Bridge (detail), 1988–89.
Jarrah railway sleepers.
Each sleeper 98.1 × 25.4 × 12.7

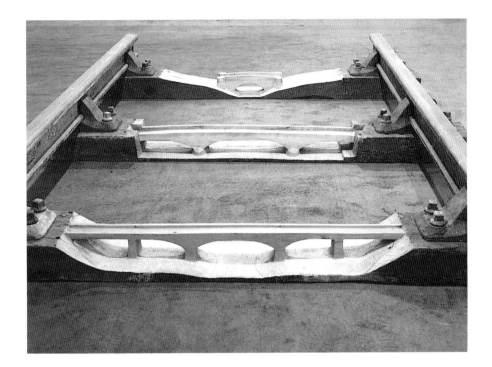

Keir Smith
Running from Eden (A River Portrait), 1988.
Jarrah railway sleepers.
Each sleeper 98.1 × 30.5 × 15.2

Keir Smith TEMPLE GARDENS

The Way of Clouds A Sculpture for Lincoln

A series of clouds made from Lincolnshire limestone, to be carved in the Cathedral Quarry and eventually sited in Temple Gardens, between the Usher Gallery and Lincoln Cathedral. The clouds are arranged as a linear bank suggesting an intermediary zone linking higher and lower regions : the idea of travelling through clouds, ascending and aspiring; perhaps encompassing the notion of pilgrimage.

An initial drawing for 'The Way of Clouds' proposed a series of symbolic objects resting on cumulus bases, a feather, a spire, rowing boat and full moon, deriving from sculptures, mainly carved on railway sleepers from the mid '80's, such as 'Last Rays for an English Rose' of 1986-7 and the 'Iron Road' of 1986. The combination of feather and cloud was used for a large independent carving 'Phoenix' of 1985-6 made for the Stoke on Trent Garden Festival. Working towards 'The Way of Clouds' has coincided with a rethinking of my sculpture where an exuberant formal complexity and combination of images has been rejected and replaced by a greater simplicity of utterance. Consequently the images from 'The Way of Clouds' are nearer to observable phenomena; cumulus type clouds, characterised, differentiated but divested of symbolic accoutrements. The spire, present in the original drawing has been expanded into a separate work, a group of towers, to be made at a later date, reflecting my growing interest in architecture, in the churches of Wren, Hawksmoor and Gibbs and more functional edifices such as lighthouses and pylons.

Clouds have been a much used image in my work throughout the 1980's culminating in the cloudscapes contained within the 'Iron Road' of 1986 and the series of rust drawings of 1988-89 entitled 'A Catalogue of Clouds'. They represent the realm of the imagination (or at least an escape from the mundane) a place of dreaming and freedom far removed from the overbearing constraints of gravity. Such images reflect my admiration for the towering skies of Turner and Constable, particularly the latter's late painting of Salisbury Cathedral, beset by lightning and redeemed by a rainbow. It is ironic that such images are realised in stone, their heaviness apparent, resonant with geology. Perhaps the image transcends matter.

Keir Smith
March 1990

Keir Smith has been commissioned by the Usher Gallery to make a
new piece, *The Way of Clouds,* to be sited in Temple Gardens, the
grounds of the Usher Gallery.

The life of clouds:
Protean.
Occasionally,
Assuming,
Perfect form.
Momentarily Classic.

Keir Smith
1990

Sue Hilder TUPHOLME ABBEY

"Experiencing the present purely is being emptied and hollow; you catch grace as
a man fills his cup under a waterfall." *Annie Dillard.* [1]

I follow the paths
through the woods
through the fields
by the river
along the shore
with my mind open
my eyes wide
and my fingers searching.

I stop along the way
to sit still and listen and see.

Sometimes my fingers find work to do
amongst the grass and leaves
the water and pebbles.

Sometimes they don't.

Sometimes it's enough to be in the place.

[1] *Pilgrim at Tinker Creek,*
Annie Dillard, Pan Books,
London, 1976.

Sue Hilder
Spate, September 1989.
Tostary Bay, Isle of Mull.
Cibachrome photograph of work
made with shale
50.8 × 66

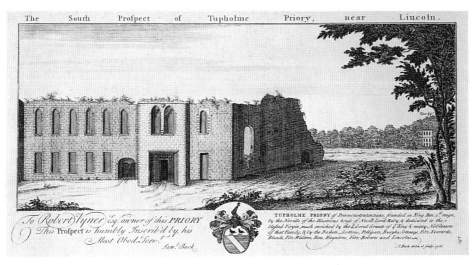

Samuel Buck, 1696 – 1779, Tupholme Abbey, 1726. Engraving.
18 x 36. Collection Usher Gallery, Lincoln.

The journey through the land
is a way of discovery and re-discovery
The traveller does not impose
but absorbs and reacts intuitively,
discovering forms and processes of balance in nature,
and re-discovering innate spiritual balance.

I go to the land to learn
not to plunder.
My work is the residue of a learning process
which involves physical and spiritual contact with land.
I seek to gain understanding
without causing disruption.
Most of the time I fail
but failing is learning.

My journey through the land
is a series of moments
when human nature and land nature
come together.
These moments are windows of perception.

Sue Hilder
March 1990

Sue Hilder is to make new work at the site of Tupholme Abbey
during the project.

Bartholomew Howlett, 1767 – 1827, Temple Bruer, published 1801. Engraving (drawn by William Alexander from a sketch by Thomas Espin). 13.8 x 18.7. Collection Usher Gallery, Lincoln.

A young artist is to be selected by open submission, to make new
work at the site of Temple Bruer, Preceptory of
the Knights Templar.

The Spirituality of Contemporary Art

Sister Wendy Beckett

MANY PEOPLE ARE AFRAID OF CONTEMPORARY ART; many people are afraid of prayer. This is in no sense a criticism. We are all afraid of the unknown or of situations where we are not in control, unless – this is the crucial point – we are absolutely certain of the good will of the one in command. We human beings are not naturally trustful. At base, we feel we can only rely totally upon ourselves, and it is the greatest mark of love we can show when we assent to commit ourselves to another. Love is wholly a question of this trust. Each side exposes itself to the power and to the weakness of the other. Prayer is exposure to the unknown mystery of God. Art demands that we surrender to the unknown power of an artist. We cannot make conditions in advance in either case. Our attitude to prayer and to the art of our own times rests on rather similar foundations.

I am speaking of the art of our own times, because that is the only art we meet in exposure, so to speak. The art of the past has its credentials already. We take no risk there, nobody is going to regard us as gullible for responding to Rembrandt or Fra Angelico. The risk rather is of revealing a failure to respond, and we must sometimes wonder how free we are, being in a society where our fellows judge our reactions and evaluate us, to being a clear, unprejudiced eye to art that has been certified by history as Great. We certainly can never see it with the innocence of its contemporaries, who had to decide for themselves how valuable to the spirit this picture or sculpture truly was. As we know, they often judged mistakenly. Van Gogh's rejection is only the most blatant example of an age's blindness to the quality of its art. The children of those who scoffed at the Impressionists and thought them hideous were loud in their contempt for Picasso, until the sheer size of his income from his work silenced even the most unimpressed. Even then, the idea persisted that Picasso was a brilliant trickster. It does not seem possible that those who thought this ever really brought themselves to look straight at what he had created. No need for us to feel superior. How straight have we looked at the art of our own time, that art that carries no credentials except its own integrity? There is no one to tell us how to respond to it. We are on our own, exposed, and hence the profound likeness to the act of prayer. Silent prayer, the prayer of the heart, cannot be learned and cannot be evaluated except in its fruits. 'By their fruits ye shall know them' holds for artists as well, but first we must taste the fruit. And to taste it, we must bring to it a clean palate, not one furred by fears and prejudices. Looking at art and looking at God have much in common.

But perhaps what is most in common is almost beyond putting into words. We accept, at least in theory, that prayer is a spiritual activity and opens our heart to the Transcendent. What we call this Transcendence is up to us. Christians say God, and so do Jews; but every religion has a sacred Name for the Divinity. If we regard this Divinity as essential Mystery, which is what Christians (and others) believe, since we are told in the New Testament that 'No one has seen the Father except the one who came from God', Jesus Himself, then this spiritual activity widens out to encompass atheists as well. They may not know the divine Name, but the very longing for Transcendence that is so deep in the human heart, the very agony of our human contingency, our need of the Ideal, all is a valid form of what the religious-minded call prayer. Some of those who know God best, and whose lives make this evident, may not know that it is God who inspires their idealism and their courage. Herbert McCabe, writing in the *Independent*, put it well. Traditionally, he says, 'the word "God" is used for God not because its meaning is thought to correspond to the nature of God, but simply as a convenient label for the ultimate, altogether incomprehensible mystery because of which things exist instead of there not being anything at all.' The meaning of prayer is to surrender in trust to this Mystery. But it is this same mystery that touches us in art. Contemplating art is a sort of anonymous prayer, a reaching out beyond the narrowness of our own limitations and entering into contact with, not the idea of God, (that flawed concept per se) but the Reality. Naming is unimportant; it is experiencing that matters.

But to experience means to give time and energy. We can no more see (in any real sense) a work of art by merely glancing and moving on, than we can hear songs from reading the record cover or catching a few notes. Thomas Hess, Director of the Metropolitan Museum in New York, said that it takes years to see a picture. The more we look, the more we are able to look, the deeper our experience becomes, the more profound our enrichment of spirit. The thing is, of course, to start, and to decide really to look and to let the work impress itself upon us. We may decide that we do not like it, but we have given it the respect that everyone's labour demands; we have judged slowly.

Speaking of God as pure and essential Mystery makes it clear that we are not to confuse spiritual art with religious art. Obviously, religious art aspires to be spiritual, but it is not a question of the artist's intentions. Religious art that is not centred enough to be 'spiritual' is distinguished by its images. They come from some definite religious faith, and they are effective to the degree to which they activate the faith of the viewer. They are springboards, they set in motion what we already know, and the devotion we already possess. But if the artist has created not just religious art but spiritual art, then these images carry us beyond what we already accept. They become luminous with a divine light, and they change us. We change ourselves if we use religious art sincerely, but we are changed by something greater than ourselves if we use spiritual art as we should.

In contemporary terms, this sort of twofold art is very rare. Art historians have gone on record as claiming that the last religious painter in this sublime sense was Georges Rouault, who died in 1958. It is understandable that this should be rare. The Religious artist (with a capital R), does not only express his own faith – this is happily not uncommon. Nor is it enough that he or she be highly gifted, because there have been artists of the greatest calibre whose religious art falls flat. (Manet is a good example.) No, the necessary condition is that the artist is compelled from the inmost depths of his or her being to body forth a vision in terms of religious imagery. It cannot be achieved by willing; it is beyond the conscious control of the creating hand. Rouault's Suffering Christ figures are almost unbearable in their intensity, unmistakably taking their rise from something absolutely fundamental to his personal being. But he was by no means the last, as it happens. Albert Herbert is another such Religious painter of genius, his biblical images thrusting their way onto the canvas or paper almost against his volition. Another Religious artist, shy, hesitant and almost evanescent on the page, is Alan Shipway. His *Buddha in the Forest* shows beautifully the non-dogmatic power of Religious spiritual art. We do not have to be Buddhist to respond to this moving work. It is almost monochrome, dark trees, pale yellow soil. The one astonishing area of colour is the small blue bird towards which the Buddha stretches his hand. But when we look at this clear brightness of blue, incredibly sweet in so dark a world-view, we begin to see that the washed-out sky is also faintly blue, and the colourless Buddha is most delicately flushed with the same heavenly blueness.

It is ourselves that we see, straying in a pathless forest, in a world where there may not be much warmth and brightness, and yet meeting, humbly, gently, almost unnoticed, the blue and winged creature that transforms our dullness into life. Shipway is sharing a vision with us. If we let the vision work upon us, we will know what it 'means', though not in words. Albert Herbert works from vision, too, and nobody has to believe that God really did speak to Moses on the mountain before they can respond to what his vision stammers forth to us. Brave and small, Moses has laboured along up to the heights, his ego dissolved in the unseen and unseeable closeness of his God. He spreads his stick-like arms to embrace that

Alan Shipway, The Buddha in the Forest, 1985. Acrylic on canvas, 92 x 73

Albert Herbert, "Moses Climbs the Mountain of God", 1982. Etching. 15.2 x 21.6

mystery, he offers himself confidently to its awesome power. Down below are those for whose sake he has made this journey. But those who stay on the ground must accept the consequences: large ego-heads quite unaffected by the divine, and a meaninglessness to their existence. Or – if we like – we could read the characters in the myth as all aspects of Moses, with the parts of himself that he did not surrender to God. We can read what 'meanings' into it that make sense so us: meaning in art is always a personal matter, up for grabs, so to speak, (provided we have taken time and trouble to arrive at what we think). But, like Buddha, Moses is us all, and the power of the art comes, not from the story, which both artists merely use, but from the vision. The vision in these two cases comes expressed in religious terms, but it may take any form that the artist's own inner truth demands of it.

There are no religious elements in the art of most of our contemporaries, not in the least out of irreverence or disdain or lack of faith, but because such a form would not be true for them. Yet their art is often as beautifully and deeply spiritual as is Herbert's or Shipway's. There are hundreds, thousands, of examples one could give, artists who draw us into a silence where we are touched by the holiness of transcedence. Sally Warner, an American, draws trees, brushwood, stone, and they are luminous with God. William Bailey, another, older American, paints jugs and kitchen vessels on a wooden table, with a sacramental strength that is overpowering. Avigdor Arikha, an Isræli, can show us a bare wall, a broom, bottles, young women, rooms and stairways or – as here – scattered *Shoes and Socks,* and the viewer signs with the wonder of what is seen. Arikha makes no attempt to glorify his shoes and socks. They lie crumpled and shabby, not even, we feel, arranged for our viewing. But the artist has seen their simple quiddity, their truth to their own nature, their materiality, as purely beautiful. His charcoal hovers around their forms with both love and reverence. David Hockney has said, and very truly, that 'all art, all creativity, comes from love'. It is the ability to share this love with us that distinguishes a painter like Arikha.

Love does not glamourise; it does not need to. What the artist sees may be a sad truth. Elizabeth Frink moulded a series in the sixties that she entitled *'Goggle Heads'*. Each is a great thickened male head, with coarse and prognathous chin and with great goggles hiding the eyes. She was at one level alluding to the gangs of youths on motor cycles that had been wreaking senseless destruction on the helpless, but on another level, she is revealing the hidden brutality of us all. We are all masked against the light of truth, lumpen heads without a function. Only love can understand this and show it as both frightening and sad. If we shudder at *Goggled Head*, it is as one accused, but not condemned. Yet it is not what 'lessons' we can draw from it that makes art spiritual, it is the actual impact of the work on a responsive psyche. We can see this most clearly in abstract art, where we must sink or swim. The art offers the intellect little standing ground. We can attribute specific meanings if we like. It is easy, for example, to see the flowing folds of Be van der Heide's work as landscape, but it is the landscape of the Spirit. We diminish the power if we try to tame it overmuch. Rothko, whose work is so deeply spiritual, became distressed if it was given precise interpretations, called 'Temple art', or seen as the holy tent of Meeting of the Old Testament. It had indeed a 'content', he insisted, but not one that could be verbalised. Jean Gibson's wall-sculptures change their patterns as the day changes, light moving silently over the rough surfaces where some urgency struggles to break into visibility. But at no time of the day or the year does the urgency take on the delineations of actuality. She leaves us free to enter into the struggle, and the sense of interior victory, the battle won from the outset, that her work sets before us. It is a temptation, perhaps, to regard abstract art as the only 'spiritual' art, and to respond in freedom to, say, the ordered magnificences of Mali Morris more than to the impotence and pathos of Marcelle Hanselaar's women, (like *'Daddy's Little Girl'*) or Eileen Cooper's mother-and-

Elizabeth Frink, Head, 1967. Bronze.

Avigdor Arikha, Shoes and Socks, 1977. Brush and Ink, 97 x 63

child icons, so primitive and so moving. We may feel we understand these images on our own terms, that they are worldly art. But the power of these artists comes from a spiritual source, their closeness to Essential Beauty, and what they show is as mysterious, as holy, as the abstractions of Morris or Gibson. The appearance differs; the power is the same, or differs only in relation to the artistic capability of each. In whatever form it comes to us, art carries within it this strange capacity to widen our narrowness and draw us further than we could ever go of ourselves.

We can so easily live in a prison of the ego, life bounded by personal anxieties, hopes, pleasures and frustrations. But we were made for liberty. The freedom need not be painfully gained, one by one. We are social beings, and no gift is ever meant only for the gifted, it is for sharing, for enriching others. Artists accept their sacred responsibility: let us also accept ours. We complete their works when we open to them, enter into their beauty or their terror, when we let them become prayer for us, as they most truly are.

Art is a Pathless Land

Malcolm Miles

IS THERE A BROKEN TRADITION of art and the "spirit"? Is this the same as the sometimes forgotten history of art in religious buildings? Can art transform a space into a place for tranquillity, which heals? Is this "peace" in the mind of the beholder reminded of an inner depth, a kind of nothingness?

In moments of intense perception which stir wonder – watching light flickering on water, or the endlessness of stars in the desert sky – or standing before works of great art – Cimabue's crucifix in S. Croce or Fra Angelico's Saint Dominic at the Foot of the Cross in S Marco, both in Florence – the conscious mind's chattering is stilled. The historical circumstances of art's production become as dust; the spectator is aware (beyond the coloured dust of the picture) of a deep space neither inside nor outside and a profound silence. This can be called the "presence" of a work of art, which we need to understand before speculating on broken traditions, because it may be found in some contemporary art unattached to organised religion, as well as in some religious art of the past. Why are some works of art able to occasion this intense feeling in the spectator, after they have survived the historical context of their making, and despite (often) the spectator's ignorance of every detail of that history?

Such feelings are more intense than the pleasure of recognition, depend on no illusion or description, no set subjects, and transcend the matter of colour or form, though conveyed by these. Similarly, the subject-matter of art, the bowls of fruit, trees and mountains, dying gods, is not where its meaning resides. A still life by Zurbaran has the same resonance as a crucifixion and may share the same content. Any image may evoke this kind of intense feeling, if permeated by a certain deep space, an equivalent for a space of the psyche, and not a description of space – a "space between" to which insight is by grace – the deep space in Fra Angelico's crucifixion: Saint Dominic adores at the foot of the cross, before the two zones of earth (ochre/umber) and sky (indigo); Christ hangs motionless in the air. The two figures, each in their sphere, are separated (actually, which in the picture's terms becomes fictionally) by time; it is still, silent, and this feeling is as much in the overall colour and disposition of the work and its mirroring of inner space, as in its figuring. The silence is the fabric of a mysterious nothingness which is, perhaps, the root of art. Can we find ourselves subsumed in the field of this indigo and ochre, here and everywhere at once without contradiction – a paradoxical wholeness? Is this the property of art to "heal"? Or is the crossing into a land beyond our individual identity too convulsive? According to Rilke: "For Beauty is nothing but beginning of terror we are just able to bear.... Every angel is terrible."

Holderlin wrote of a void in which it seems we have lost all things, and of one in which it seems we have found all things; Freud described the feeling of the mystic, a feeling accessible also to the non-religious, as being subsumed like a drop in the ocean: the "oceanic". It may be that underlying our deepest responses to culture, and only partly mediated by our immediate culture, is a recognition of a paradoxical inner space.

In the absence of faith (an absence of imagination), psychology has assumed much of the mediative role of organised religion, and art's subjects tend to be secular. This does not detract from "spiritual" art; the secular is not opposed to the spiritual, and the tradition is debased not by the secular, nor the invention of personal privacy, but by materialism.

Psychology is now one means of access to myth, that territory once shared visually in public art, not least to the myth of thresholds. D W Winnicott has written simply and compellingly on the "space" between infant and mother:

> "I have tried to work out where cultural experience is located, and I have tentatively made this formulation: that it starts in the potential space between a child and the mother when experience has produced in the child a high degree of confidence in the mother, that she will not fail to be there if suddenly needed." [1]

By living in a "creative" sphere (of imagination) the infant can set up a "potential space" between the self and the mother, which may be symbolised by some "transitional" (going across thresholds), object, such as a blanket or soft toy, or in later life a Beethoven quartet:

> "It is a first symbol, and it stands for confidence in the union of the baby and mother.... It must be lost in the process of the introduction of the Reality Principle, but in health we devise ways and means of recapturing the feeling of meaningfulness that comes from creative living." [2]

The infant, developing, seeks selfness, independent life, the natural process of individuation. This necessarily means growing apart from the mother in whose womb the infant knew only the one fact of one world of self and other together,

[1] The Concept of a Healthy Individual, D W Winnicott, 1967.

[2] Living creatively, D W Winnicott, 1970.

[92]

and accepting negative feelings against the mother, being destructive (as Bataille says infant drawing symbolises) yet not destroying, for, at the same time, there is a counter-desire, not for individuality, but for unity, to be merged into everything else and cancel the separation (fall). Either extremity in isolation is neurosis:

> "...in health there is no separation, because in the space-time area between the child and the mother, the child (and so the adult) lives creatively." [3]

Imaginative space (of creative, psychic, or bodily, play) is that void in which all is lost and found and the mother (or otherness) is here and not here, a paradox of unity and separation – the root of art is in this "space between".

A more radical idea is that art and religious feeling share a common root: that the longing of the soul for union with (distant and hardly knowable) the god is expresseed similarly to and derived commonly from the longing of the grown infant for union with (distanced) the mother. The comparison does not damage the preciousness of either feeling. Eckhart wrote of the need to empty out all the clutter of the self in order to know God, which is like undoing the process of individuation to be reunited in primal oneness, made whole, that is, healed.

If this is so, it offers a foundation for an art of the spiritual, which may be accessible, either directly or by mediation, to all, and goes some way to explain, apart from dry notions of talent and skill, the compelling "presence" of some pictures. It also relieves us of the need to bemoan the loss of a tradition of religious art, since art arising from the "potential space" is not absent today, and never will be because it is rooted in the most essential aspect of the "human condition". Indeed, a culture entirely devoid of vehicles for this content would indicate a dead society. Ours is a fragmented society, but not without healing of sorts.

Let us return to our first questions: Is there a broken tradition of art and the "spirit"? Is this the same as the sometimes forgotten history of art in religious buildings, or the potency of art to transform a space into a place for tranquillity, which heals?

All previous societies have expressed a religious view of life through sacred art: Osiris is resurrected in the mysteries of his painted temples; Christ and the Mother of God stand in the mosaic-walls of Byzantium, and the gilded dome is a metaphor of heaven, as in the apse of S Fosca on Torcello in the Venetian Lagoon: the figure becomes space within the solid gold of the dome; the gold flickers and dissolves in the light. The figure is a Christian form of the ancient sky goddes and great mother, still meaningful to us through our response to the deep feeling of space, our unconscious recognition of the "potential space". Perhaps to contemplate such

[3] 1967 op cit.

images heals, makes us whole, at least in our psyche (which is part of our body). This does not mean that the society amidst which such works were created was any more unified or free of conflict than our own, though there was a unifying spiritual idea in its language of building and imaging, stronger than the romantic gloss of its representation in the art of the nineteenth century revivals – the gilded citadels, meadows ever green and bowers bedewed are a dream, but so, according to Calderon, is life, and even the dreams are a dream. Our dream is loss, broken things.

To portray a broken tradition is to project our own fragmented minds; the past is gilded and lost, like infancy or life within the womb, and the present is miserable. It is too easy to leave it at that and become nostalgic. Yet our psyche is that of previous generations, only mediated by history, not changed. The myths of past societies are still accessible to those who seek them, and writers such as Mircea Eliade and Marina Warner show this. To work from the tradition does not mean to copy it any more than slavish invention guarantees newness: a work will be of its maker and in a language of its time, just as what is made by hand is "personal", yet it may also partake of something beyond that, a myth which emerges as less conscious states of psyche influence the imagery and it is permeated by an underlying "ground". The tradition of pictorial space is the visual form of the poetic idea "What remains of the Beloved?" cited by Robert Graves, a coming to terms with the human condition of loss – Saint Dominic separated from the god, the infant grown (up) apart from the mother, seeking oneness – reconciled in pictures. It is also our attempt to come to terms with death, losing identity, being finally (as previously) subsumed. Artists still work from this state of mind; how could they else?

Some examples will show different ways of doing this:
Stefan Ramniceanu re-invents the imagery of the Orthodox church through contemporary, abstracted "icons". As a Romanian under the oppression of the Ceaucescu regime he, like some other artists, turned to paintings of churches as a form of carefully coded dissent, but his work goes beyond the expedient. Like Horia Bernia, he reworked the image of the church banner, in encrustations of paint which turn the picture from description to object. Some of the layers of paint-surface are scraped back, and the work takes on a damaged quality, accumulation and decay, adding and taking away, that movement across and between states of a transitional object.

In a more recent "polyptich" a field of gold is surrounded by fragments, as an icon in its frame of Saints' lives; within the gold is a fragment, figure or hand, standing as thing and space in a paradoxical relation with the ground – this is a metaphor for the space between self and encompassing mother-world. The central painted section of this picture reads (both female figure and hand) as in the Mother's hand which holds the child, in the icons called in Greek Philousa. The feeling of damage to the overall picture surface is more than effect, and the scraping back of the body of paint emphasises, here and there, the ambiguity.

In contrast but with an equally strong sense of the "space between", Craigie Aitchison creates a spiritual dimension through thin and luminous colour, and regards himself (regardless of subject matter) as a religious artist. His sources are Pre-Raphælitism, Giotto and Fra Angelico, and Catholicism. He has painted crucifixions since an early landscape of Scotland, including a solitary telegraph pole, was assumed to be one. Perhaps unconsciously it was a reworking of the crucifixions he had seen in Italy. His skies are zoned, often in the earlier works indigo, adding to the loneliness of scant, white Christs. In these pictures, colour is light and space, above all space. The same is true of his still life paintings and those of models in the studio. The paintings have an extraordinary stillness and exactness.

The indigo skies are clearly reminiscent of Fra Angelico, but there is also a feeling (found in fin de siecle painting) of the thresholds of day, dawn or twilight, through the close tones of colour zones. Vuillard was his first enthusiasm and this survives in these juxtapositions, but what permeates most is the silence, and sometimes the alone-ness into which the spectator may project loneliness. Is the myth of the dying god still something that can be shared? Perhaps the metaphor of pictorial space (the colour-space of light playing in darkness) is what lends it universality. These are unusual pictures, in that to describe them as "beautiful" is adequate.

It is relatively easy to think of pictorial space in terms of painting, but how do such feelings take form in sculpture?

Peter Randall-Page became a stone carver out of a sense of wonder at natural things. He recalls:

> "I remember as a child going for long walks. The pleasure of nature was really strong and intuitive. The incredible perfection of everything natural gave a sense of an underlying law. This was a primary influence which came before looking at art. My interest in art is in its potential as a vehicle for celebration of these feelings.

He made carvings of shell forms for Common Ground in Dorset, and endangered species for Year of the Environment:

Craigie Aitchison, 1987 – 89. Crucifixion II. Oil on canvas. 172.7 x 144.8. Courtesy The Albemarle Gallery.

Stefan Ramniceanu, Church Banner, c1986.

"I wanted the work to be still and quiet in mood, like life in a dormant or contained form...a vessel for life.

These sculptures give form to an emotion of unity-and-separation which is the same as the root of pictorial space:

"From quite early on, I felt aware that although human beings are obviously part of nature, we have a painful sense of detachment from the rest of the natural world. Our consciousness separates us but we are obviously part of that world as well. A desire to reconcile this sense of estrangement has been a driving force behind my work.

Peter Randall-Page, Still Life, 1988. Kilkenny limestone. 167.7

Estrangement is the primal wound that will not heal, separating the soul from that which is concealed by the threshold on which Rilke's angels stand, or by a "cloud of unknowing". Art can "unconceal" some layers but its potency resides in mystery and in play. What is true of this now is unchanged from earlier societies but may be expressed in a different set of codes. At the same time, as image of a state before estrangement, the Mother and Child remains an element in a common wealth of symbols, open to all who come in humility and simplicity, in a way always what Malcolm Lowry describes as "the Madonna for those who have no-one them with".

To return to our questions: the tradition of spiritual art is broken, and we live in a society of division and alienation, but perhaps people always have, and the question "What remains of the Beloved?" touches both our sense of mortality and our estrangement through reality.

Art has "presence" in as much as it conveys a "space between" – the potential space described by Winnicott, and this tradition is renewed today as ever. It is also something which, because it emerges, is unconcealed, from the un-conscious, is something which can be shared. Can it heal? Ask the Fisher-king or the drowned Phonecian. Yet their answers will be impossible to translate, and the land they inhabit has no paths. "Therefore I will leave on one side everything I can think."

The Abstract Sacred

Don Cupitt

IS THERE SUCH A THING as an art that is both genuinely modern and genuinely religious? I believe there is, and I shall describe its typical mood and style as the Abstract Sacred. The Abstract Sacred is not quite the personal God of the older Western tradition, nor is it quite the Void of Buddhism. It is somewhere between the two. But it is not a substance, not a thing. It cannot be represented directly. It hasn't even got an iconography of its own. To people who are familiar with the older tradition of religious artefacts that had to follow strictly-defined iconographical rules in order to be readable, the Abstract Sacred must seem very paradoxical. I need to explain what this new religious art is, and how it arose.

The clue to understanding what has happened to religious art in modern times is the curious and easily-overlooked fact that our present notion of art only dates back as far as the middle of the eighteenth century. As part of the general Enlightenment modernization of the culture the various fine arts, *les beaux arts* (painting, sculpture, poetry, dance, music, architecture), were for the first time all grouped together. This brought into being Art with a capital A, newly-enthroned as the highest-ranking cultural pursuit. Art was defined in terms of its relation to the creativity of the human beings who produced it and the sensibility of the other human beings who enjoyed it. The new word 'aesthetics' was coined, by the philosopher Baumgarten, for theory of art – meaning, roughly, the science of the way artworks affect our sensibility.

Art thus came to be understood in radically humanistic terms. There developed a cult of human creativity, and of pride in one's own country's artistic traditions. Art was classified into national schools. It became something to be exhibited free of charge in public national galleries, which became like shrines dedicated to the human spirit. Art was taught in academies, its history began to be constructed and it was theorized about by critics and philosophers. Art was good for you. It was also expensive, and if you were a rich and important person it was your duty to have a cultivated taste in it.

The various objects assembled in the new galleries and museums, however, had in many cases not exactly been made for this new treatment that they were receiving. They had been made under earlier conditions, when the new ideas about

Art and human creativity did not yet exist. Christian objects, in particular, had originally been made by craftsmen for Church or devotional use. In the Christian era God was the only Creator, and the word artist, if used at all, was used pretty much as we now use the word craftsman. Art was not for Art's sake, and certainly not for its effect on people's feelings. It had a religious function, aiding prayer, embellishing worship and glorifying God.

Because of all this, the older Christian works looked ill at ease in the new public galleries. An icon or an altarpiece, made by a monk to be prayed through – that is, as a tool by which to relate yourself to the sacred Being portrayed – becomes a totally different object when it is removed to a secular gallery and viewed by the public as a work of religious art and as an expression of the faith of a bygone age.

From all this it follows that our very definition of Art has for over two centuries been post-Christian. Some time around the year 1700, give or take a generation or so either way, the Great Tradition of Christian culture came to an end. The Enlightenment subsequently reshaped Western culture around the human being. Art was redefined, as we have seen. 'Man', producer and consumer, creator and experiencer, was now the subject. Art was the product of the creative person's self-expression. Art gave rise to special feelings of pleasure, harmony and sublimity in the eyes and ears of people of taste.

To fit them into this new cultural set-up, the older Christian artefacts had to be completely reinterpreted. In the process, and not surprisingly, religion too was rethought in terms of the human subject. People began to talk for the first time about 'religious experience', 'religious feeling' and 'mysticism'. Religion was becoming a human function, a mode of the human sensibility.

The upshot of this is that religious art for us moderns is no longer the old ecclesiastical art, defined in terms of the patron who commissioned it, the iconography it obeyed and the religious function it served. Religious art has broken loose: it is now any sort of art that arouses religious feelings in the contemplative spectator. The spectator is no longer quite using the art object according to canonical rules and *as religion*, but rather is receptive to its effect upon the feelings *as religious Art*. Because of this shift, an altarpiece that once stood in a church and focussed the prayers of the faithful may now be aesthetically enjoyed in a gallery in good conscience. You can have entirely creditable religious feelings in response to it, even though it has been drastically torn out of the old sacred realm for which it was originally made. In just the same way, people nowadays listen to a setting of the Mass performed in a concert hall, and visit churches as monuments of religious architecture. Furthermore, because religion and religious art are now defined in terms of our own feeling-response to them, and therefore are seen in much less immediate and dogmatically-exclusive terms than formerly, our taste can range widely. We can and do get religious pleasure from a vast range of materials, from other faiths and periods, that might once have been denounced as heathen idols. We are no longer iconoclastic; that is, we no longer react with religious revulsion and horror to other people's religious images. Instead we enjoy them – as religious Art.

However, we pay a price for this catholicity of taste and enjoyment. In order to enjoy the religious artefacts of the past, we have had to learn to read them historically as datable products of evolving human stylistic traditions. For example, when we view the window tracery or the rib vaulting in a medieval church, we date it and place it in an historical sequence. But this very manoeuvre by which we interpret the old Christian tradition and make it accessible to ourselves also prevents us from continuing it. For the old iconography no longer conducts us directly to sacred Beings in the heavenly world; it merely stands at a certain point in an historical series. This in turn means that modern religious art has to be very different in type from the Christian art of earlier times.

Vincent van Gogh, in the asylum at Saint Rémy in the Autumn of 1889, was thinking much about religious subjects – for example, Christ in Gethsemane. But as everyone knows he ended up leaving Christ out, and painting only the writhing olive trees, because a painting of Christ wouldn't succeed in being a portrayal of Christ himself. It would merely be a parody or a variation upon a familiar theme from the history of art. We would not be led by van Gogh's work to think directly about Christ; we would merely find ourselves thinking about the long line of earlier representations of the *Agony in the Garden* in the history of Christian art. So van Gogh left the human figures out of the painting, and wrote to Emile Bernard: 'One can try to give an impression of anguish without aiming straight at the historic garden of Gethsemane' (21 December 1889). He similarly leaves Christ out of the *Raising of Lazarus* (May 1890). And all this was consistent with a long-declared policy. The celebrated *Potato Eaters* of April 1885 reworks the Supper at Emmaus as a simple peasant meal, and the *Still Life with Open Bible* of October 1885 shows Zola's grim secular novel *Joie de Vivre* as the true modern counterpart of the 53rd chapter of the Book of the Prophet Isaiah. Messianic suffering is now dispersed into general human suffering.

Van Gogh is saying then that, paradoxically, if a modern work of art is to be authentically religious today, it cannot be religious in the old sense. It must look secular. The agony of the olive trees, the peasant meal, and the afflicted woman of the drawing *Sorrow* must be enough for us. And that is part of what I mean by the Abstract Sacred. After the Enlightenment we found that the very moves by which we had made the old religious iconographies intelligible to ourselves also made it

Sir Jacob Epstein, Lazarus, 1947. Hoptonwood stone. 289 × 69. Reproduced by permission of the Warden and Fellows, New College, Oxford.

impossible for us to continue them *as religion*. We had irreversibly become like those eighteenth-century ladies and gentlemen who clucked over ruined abbeys, grottoes and hermits. We are all of us now Heritage-Christians, tourists of religion, looking respectfully at the lovingly-preserved relics of a lost past. We quickly fall into the mood of those people who after much searching decide that the only non-embarassing Christmas card they can find to send is a reproduction of a medieval manuscript illumination. Among such people, culture-conservatives, nostalgia for faith is only too easily mistaken for faith itself.

Our present argument however suggests that an authentic modern religious art must not be in any way revivalist. It must break with historicism and nostalgia for tradition. That is surely why a good deal of high Modernist and Abstract Expressionist art does strike people today as being authentically religious. Purged of subjectivity and romantic nostalgia, and without any reference to established iconographies, it is able to acquire a special kind of impersonal and objective weight and presence. As is well known, Mondrian and Kandinsky both hoped that through abstraction it might be possible for Art once more to communicate spiritual values. How successful they themselves were is perhaps disputable; but for me and surely for many other people the great works of Jackson Pollock, Barnett Newman, Ad Rhinehart, Mark Rothko, Yves Klein and others are highly religious. They are expressions of what I am calling the Abstract Sacred.

This however is a new kind of Sacred, for these works are not like the old Eastern Christian icons. They are post-platonic. They are not windows upon eternity. You do not use them as openings into the supernatural world. They do not point to anything else. They are flat, really flat. This Sacred is abstract in two senses: there is no imagery, and there is no other-world-beyond. Instead you stop on this surface, a little perhaps like a Buddhist meditating on a flower. Substance dissolves away, and the ego dissolves away. There is only this, the Abstract Sacred, flux, Void, This-ness, secularity, dispersal.

Notoriously, such an art has proved extremely stressful and costly for the artist to produce. But modern religion just *is* costly, as is perhaps indicated in a different way by the work of Käthe Kollwitz. Kollwitz was active in Berlin during the first forty-odd years of this century. She is a strong humanist, who portrays anonymous human suffering with a very fiercely controlled grief. Somehow she will not allow suffering to be in any way whatever justified, idealized, transfigured or altered. Sometimes she can seem sentimental, but at least in her most austere works *the total absence of any religious consolation is itself what makes the work religious!* That is the paradox of twentieth-century religious naturalism. The Abstract Sacred demands truth to things as they are, and a rigorous refusal to accept the lie of

Vincent Van Gogh, Sorrow, April 1882. Pencil, pen and ink. 44.5 x 27. The Garman Ryan Collection, Walsall Museums and Art Gallery, Walsall Leisure Services.

[101]

otherworldiness. We must be saints of the earth.

The paradoxes are multiplying. Van Gogh finds that if it is to be effectively Christian nowadays, art must leave out Christ himself. To be truly religious, it must be 'flat', entirely of this world and quite unconsoled. The Abstract Sacred gets its religious weight from its very repudiation of the supernatural, a point eloquently made in the work of Richard Long. When people compare Long's works of landscape art with megalithic monuments, the comparision only draws attention to the uncompromising horizontality of Long's work. From Babylonian zigguats and Stonehenge to Victorian spires, through almost five millenia, religion had pointed upwards towards a higher world. Long's chosen materials, rocks and mud, stood at the bottom of the old Chain of Being. They could not be more than a launch-pad for the soul. Long, however, really does want us to stop at them. They are not to be used as mere jumping-off points: in Long's work the Abstract Sacred stays on the land surface, and we should stay there too.

Richard Long, *Six Stone Circles*, 1981, Delabole Slate. Diameter 7.32 m. Courtesy Anthony d'Offay Gallery

Long makes almost no provision for the conservation of his work. He produces little in the way of saleable commodity-art. His works are made as he passes by and then left to fade, so that they can be read as symbols of human transience. How are they able to give us such a strong sense of the Sacred? By, I think, their austerity and impersonality, and by their matter-of-fact acceptance of their own transience. They seem to speak to us of an enduring unnameable Background against which our brief life is acted out. But this Background, this Abstract Sacred, must not be reified, nor must it be thought of as an Eternal One. It is something for which we have no developed vocabulary, but of which art has made us aware. It may be a starting-point for the religion of the future.

I must thank Peter Fuller, for giving me the stimulus to write this piece when I heard him lecture and saw how completely I disagreed with him.

Visual Art in Churches in England in Recent Times

Keith Walker

ST MATTHEW'S CHURCH, Northampton celebrated its fiftieth anniversary in 1943. The vicar, the Rev Walter Hussey, conceived the idea of involving the arts. His scheme was novel for he looked for the best in the diversity of the arts and, but for discrimination and courage, all might have foundered. His achievement was supremely successful and the tone of this brief essay is set by the observations of Sir Kenneth Clark writing to Hussey after seeing the maquettes for one of the commissions, namely, Henry Moore's *Madonna and Child*, "I consider him the greatest living sculptor and it is of the utmost importance that the Church should employ artists of first-rate talent instead of the mediocrities usually employed…his sketches promise that this will be one of his finest works. I am sure that it will shed great lustre on your church". [1]

Hussey's work at Northampton broke a threshold that had been sealed virtually since the mid-nineteenth century when the Earl of Shrewsbury supported Pugin. [2] An exception may be claimed for the work of Fr Bernard Walke who invited, in 1920, a number of artists from Newlyn to paint the lives of the Cornish saints in his tiny church of St Hilary, near Penzance. But none of the artists were remarkable and even Roger Fry is remembered today as a critic rather than an artist. Dean Eric Milner-White had a deep sensitivity to spiritual and artistic facts but his innovative work in the visual arts was very slight. The Church of the Ascension, Bitterne Park, Southampton accepted his recommendation of Nicholson for its new stained glass. The achievement is moderate and the idiom late Victorian. In his enthronement address in 1929 Bishop George Bell expressed the wish to foster the relation between the arts and the Church. His patronage in drama had been magnificent, but a man who could describe Picasso as "the devil incarnate" was likely to have a limited appreciation of visual art. A notable effort lay in the decoration of Berwick church, in the diocese of Chichester. Most of the work was dedicated in 1943. The artists were members of the Bloomsbury Group. Duncan Grant painted a *Christ in Glory*, the *Four Seasons* and a *Crucifixion*. Vanessa Bell painted an *Annunciation* and *Nativity*. Quentin Bell painted *The Parable of the Wise and Foolish Virgins* and *Six Sacraments* and a *Virgin and Child* altar cloth. Sir John

[1] Walter Hussey, *Patron of Art*, Weidenfeld & Nicholson 1985, p.30.

[2] Sir Kenneth Clark, "Dean Walter Hussey – A Tribute to His Patronage of the Arts", *Chichester 900*, Chichester Cathedral, 1975, p.68f.

[104]

Rothenstein, the then Director of the Tate Gallery declared them "among the best paintings" to be made for any English church this century. But we have only to think of Stanley Spencer's brilliant murals in Burghclere Chapel to realise how subjective was Sir John's judgement. [3] Not the least problem was the lack of coherent liturgical order in the positioning of the paintings. Bell also commissioned and encouraged the muralist, Hans Feibusch, who painted the *Baptism of Christ* (1951) in Chichester Cathedral, a *Pilgrim's Progress* in St Elizabeth's Church, Eastbourne, a *Christ Appearing to the Disciples* (1952) for All Hallow's Church, Wellingborough, and work in Bell's private chapel. His work breaks away from the exhausted Victorian vein of inspiration with figures vital yet sacred. Feibusch was a learned man with a deep knowledge of Christian doctrine and iconography. He could not quite rise to the demands of sacred art in the twentieth century but he understood the desperate need. Hussey was to read to his Parochial Church Council from Feibusch's *Mural Painting* words that may be quoted here: "let churches be decorated by such men as Rouault or Graham Sutherland, in whom there is fire...To see the way some of our best church and cathedral builders decorate their work with nursery emblems, golden stars, chubby Christmas angels, lilies, lambs and shepherds, insipid sculptures and paintings of a silly, false naivety, one wonders in what world they live. The men who come home from the war, and all the rest of us, have seen too much horror and evil...Only the most profound, tragic, moving, sublime vision can redeem us". [4]

Hussey came to Moore through seeing his war-time drawings and conferring with art historians. He approached Moore and asked him about the subject of a Madonna and Child and whether Moore "would *believe* in the subject". The answer was significant, "Yes, I would. Though whether or not I should agree with your theology, I just do not know. I think it is only through our art that we artists can come to understand your theology". [5] He reflected later (1943) to Hussey on the difference between secular and religious art: "It's not easy to describe in words what this difference is, except by saying in general terms that the 'Madonna and Child' should have an austerity and a nobility and some touch of grandeur (even hieratic aloofness) which is missing in the 'everyday' 'Mother and Child' idea". [6]

Moore's statue was unveiled in 1944. It stood on a two feet high plinth and was rather more than life-size. It is carved in brown Hornton stone. The Madonna looks down the aisle to the approaching visitor and the Child looks towards him on arrival. Together with the early Renaissance influence Richard Cork discerns the effect of Masaccio's *Virgin and Child* in particular. There is also a debt to primitive art noticed no doubt by Graham Greene who observed sarcastically, "It reeks of comparative religion". [7] Such influences, however, are controlled by Moore's

Henry Moore, Madonna and Child, 1943 – 4. Honiton stone. Height 151. Reproduced by permission of St. Matthew's Church, Northampton.

[3] Richard Shone, *The Berwick Church Paintings*, Towner Art Gallery, Eatbourne, 1969.

[4] *Patron of Art,* pp54 – 5.

[5] Ibid, p.24.

[6] Ibid, p.33.

[7] John Rothenstein, *Time's Thievish Progress* Cassell, 1970, p.170.

expressive ability to portray Mary the Mother of God and Jesus the Saviour of the World. Tom Driberg, who may have read Moore's introduction in the Jubilee booklet for St Matthew's, reported that the statue had "something primaeval and eternal: it is hieratic yet human; it has intense dignity, and its beauty grows on you the longer you look at it." [8] Not everyone agreed with Driberg. Sir Alfred Munning, President of the Royal Academy, chose the occasion of his Presidential Address to the Royal Academy in 1949 to criticise modern art and singled out Moore's *Madonna and Child* for special abuse. This led to correspondence in the national press reported by Hussey in a chapter headed "Sound and Fury". [9] The problem modern art can create apparently afflicts the art world itself as well as the Church.

Hussey's second great commission in the visual arts was dedicated in 1946. Graham Sutherland's *Crucifixion* stands in the South Transept, opposite Moore's statue, and complementary to it. He had intimated to Hussey that as between the detached and hieratic and psychological and real (but not necessarily naturalistic) approaches, he inclined to the latter. The result vindicates his approach. Sutherland is indebted to El Greco and Grunewald, but also to pictures of concentration camp prisoners. His Christ is caught in unspeakable death agony but seems removed from mundane actuality, living on some eternal plane of being. The composition of chest and belly is such that is is both a tortured man and the tongued visage of a ghoulish cat or demon. The painful wreath of thorns is at the same time a half-dislodged golden crown, the thorns being stars. The background is suggestive of what Eric Newton called the "no-man's land of the imagination". [10]

Hussey's curate, Methuen Clarke, became eventually vicar of All Hallows Church, Wellingborough. Following Hussey's lead he commissioned Feibusch to make a mural and became what John Piper called "an inspired commissioner of stained glass". [11] Piper and Reyntiens did work there (1961-9), Jean Barrilet made a St Crispin window, and the brilliant Celtic artist, Evie Hone, made a magnificent window of three lights depicting the Old Covenant, the Saviour of the World, and the Church, in a series of representational images (1955). Her work came to a peak in the East Window of Eton College Chapel. The Crucifixion is depicted in the upper lights and the Last Supper in the lower. Early medieval influence is strong in the elongated figures and brilliant colouring. Acceptance of this work may have caused Dean Milner-White to resign his Fellowship of the College, but the standard *The Study of Liturgy*, edited by C. Jones, G. Wainwright and E. Yarnold (1978) discriminatingly uses it for a cover illustration.

Coventry Cathedral was consecrated in 1962. The inspired architect was Basil Spence, who managed the whole enterprise for which division of opinion remains

Graham Sutherland, Crucifixion, 1946. Oil on hardboard. 243.8 × 228.5 Reproduced by permission of St. Matthew's Church, Northampton.

[8] Patron of Art, p.47.

[9] Ibid, ch.5.

[10] Ibid, p.64.

[11] Ibid, Introduction.

[106]

to this day (Basil Spence gives his view in *Phoenix at Coventry*, Collins, 1964. Recent views are summarised in J. Thomas, *Coventry Cathedral*, 1987). The whole and parts are functional and symbolic reminding us that whilst there is art in churches, churches can be art. The West Wall is made of glass, engraved in splendid angels and saints by John Hutton. Through this we see as far as the East end where the largest tapestry in the world dominates the interior, Graham Sutherland's 40′ x 60′ *Christ in Majesty*. The positioning of the tapestry is liturgically excellent. A supreme and triumphant truth is spoken from the right location. The colouring is splendid and Spence may be correct in believing that the symbols for the four Evangelists are the finest in the tradition of Christian art. The Byzantine head of Christ is impressively dignified and regally compassionate. The hesitation comes with the tightness of the whole composition, compared with the preliminary sketches, and with the torso. The figure may be sitting or standing and the bulbous clothing may be mistaken for the abdomen of an insect or an egg. But a symbol should not confuse, however divergent interpretations might be. The Tapestry was superbly woven by Pinton Frères, Aubusson, France. At that time English weavers could not rise to the challenge.

The Piper and Reyntiens Baptistry window in the south nave wall consists of 198 rectangular lights, each 50″ x 21″. The abstract pattern is made of primary colours, a large pool of whites and golds in the centre have above them celestial blues and purples and beneath earth colours of reds and greens. The window, 81′ x 51′ has won universal praise as a masterpiece of sacred art, its abstract pattern wisely avoiding competition with the figurative tapestry.

Epstein's bronze statue of *St Michael and the Devil* was one of his last major works. The strong, radiant figure of St Michael dominates the repulsive, defeated devil. The bronze is a metaphor of the Coventry achievement and enduring symbol of the Christian life. Epstein was a sculptor of genius with a deep spiritual awareness. His ecclesiastical commissions were, however, few – *Christ in Majesty* (1953-4) at Llandaff Cathedral, *Lazarus* (1948) at New College Chapel, Oxford, *Madonna and Child* (1952) for Heythrop College, Cavendish Square, London. They are all sculptures of a high order, but it seems Epstein's Jewishness and modernity restrained potential ecclesiastical patrons.

The first commission of Hussey as Dean of Chichester (1955-77) was the refurbishment of the St Mary Magdalen Chapel. The Cathedral Architect, Robert Potter, supervised the work, himself designing the altar. Geoffrey Clarke made the bronze altar rails, free-standing candlesticks and altar book rest, and Graham Sutherland painted a *Noli me Tangere* (1961), placed centrally on the altar. This chapel is seen from the west end of the Cathedral. From a distance the visitors see a splash of reds, whites and greens, suggestive of life. Nearby we see the relatively uncommon gospel scene of the Resurrected Jesus telling Mary not to touch him as he has not yet ascended. She bows low, voluptuous still. Christ begins to mount stairs traversing the picture, long arm pointing upward. His yellow hat is both the rough hat of a gardener and a halo.

Piper's High Altar tapestry was dedicated in 1966. Its brilliant colours relieved the dull and gloomy sanctuary. Piper explained the iconography as follows: "The scheme is The Trinity (three central panels) represented by an equilateral triangle among flames, and related to this, symbols of The Father (a white light), The Son (a Tau Cross), and The Holy Spirit (a flame-like wing); and the flanking panels, two on each side, The Elements at the top (Earth, Air, Fire, Water), and The Evangelists below them – St Matthew (winged man), St Mark (winged lion), St Luke (winged ox), and St John (winged eagle). The tapestry was woven by Pinton Frères, at Felletin, near Aubusson". [12] When the final sketch was shown to the Chapter the Archdeacon pointed out that God the Father was not represented, Piper having assumed that the triangle basically represented him. Piper discovered the way to amend the error after visiting Grunewald's great Resurrection painting. [13]

Hussey was also innovative in other textiles, Piper and Ceri Richards were both employed to design copes and eucharistic vestments, making a welcome break with the usual dull ecclesiastical designs.

In 1978 Hussey's final act of patronage for the Church was unveiled in the Arts to the Glory of God (Psalm 150) window, designed by Marc Chagall and made by Charles Marq. The dominant colour is red with little vignettes illustrating various arts leading up to King David and the Tablet of the Law. Chagall is a twentieth century master painter and stained glass designer. At the outset of Hussey's negotiations there was only one Chagall window in England, at All Saints' Church, Tudely, Kent. later that whole church was completed with wonderful glass from the same source. The Church of the Ascension, Stirchley also has a Chagall and Marq window.

Holy Spirit Window, 1988. Designed by *Cecil Collins*, made by *Patrick Reyntiens*. West Window, All Saints Church, Basingstoke.

It is significant that one of Hussey's greatest acts of patronage at Chichester finds no mention in his slightly self-congratulatory *Patron of Art*. Cecil Collins' *The Icon of Divine Light* (1973) is the altar frontal in St Clement's Chapel. Hussey may have been unsure about the iconic, universal symbolism, but if so I believe he was mistaken. The icon is in gold and yellow colours. The central image is of a sun or sun-flower with radiating rays or petals. Stars or tiny flowers surround the central image. It is an expression of Paradise conceived as a garden or the empyrean. The imaginative and technical effort to produce this work must have been enormous.

[12] Chichester Cathedral, Picton Visitor's Guide, 1971.

[13] Patron of Art, ch.12.

The loving, expansive central image with its personal centre imaged as a face makes the piece wholly illustrative of Christian doctrine, while persons of other faiths or none can respond profoundly to it.

I became vicar of All Saints' Church, Basingstoke in 1983. The church, built by Temple Moore in 1917 is Victorian Gothic and one of the finest in Hampshire. The first new work of art to be commissioned was a bronze *Head of Christ* (1983) by Elizabeth Frink. At the time it was the only piece of worthy sculpture in a prosperous town of 100,000 population. Some of the best theology is uttered by artists, and such an utterance is this Frink bronze. It is a head of completeness. Massively strong and contemplatively intelligent the male power is partly transformed into feminine tenderness seen from the side. All the suffering of some profound shock is gathered below the eyes, whilst the flame-like triangle of the forehead is suggestive of divinity. It is placed in the baptistry, above the font.

Plain glass filled the windows at the west end of the church, one large, two small. Agreeing with Patrick Reyntiens that "Arguably Cecil Collins is the most important metaphysical artist to have emerged in England since Blake". [14] I was anxious to continue his relation with the Church, despite the shock of disappointment over the failure of his astonishing *Icon of Divine Love* to find a place in Chichester Cathedral in 1978. He visited All Saints' Church and absorbed quickly the serene atmosphere of the place. As he contemplated the west end of the church he affirmed that some fructification was taking place deep within. The eventual result was a perception of a scheme for all the windows which, he said, would only be a revealing of what had always been there. Lack of funds meant that the scheme was realised in two stages, the small windows on either side of the great West Window were completed in 1985 and the central large window in 1988.

The theme is that of the Holy Spirit, Collins taking his inspiration from the atmosphere of the church and the positioning of the West Window above the *Head of Christ* and font (see *Mark* 1, 9-11). Each side window has two adjacent lights. These are filled with gold, yellow and white glass depicting attendant angels. An angel fills each light, each slightly different from the other. Between these lights and above them is a smaller light and this is filled with a flaming sun. The source is Byzantine and the angels as beautiful and authentic as any I have seen. Each holds a disc in the region of the chest. Within the disc is a heart and within the heart an open eye. The angels are understood to be messengers and mediators between the onlooker and God symbolised as the sun.

All that is in these windows is caught up and glorified in the central large window. The severe masculine shape of the window frame confirmed Collins' wish to find a circular feminine form appropriate for the Holy Spirit. At the centre

14 The Tablet, 27 July 1974.

we find a serene face which is also the sun. Radiating outwards are heart-shaped rays with eyes. Beyond these are wheeling angels set in the empyrean. The expanding circles are eventually broken off by the constricting window frame suggestive of the infinitude of God. These magnificent designs were made brilliantly into stained glass by Patrick Reyntiens.

Had space permitted I would have wished to dilate upon the work of Thetis Blacker, Peter Ball, Beryl Deane, Marianne Fortonnatto and others, but indication enough has been given, I hope, of some of the best work to be found in English churches since the forties. It has been a period when the Church has definitely if incompletely recovered its relation with the arts for the glory of God. The conviction remains that art is not idle decoration but integral to the effort of the Church to minister God. Words are one medium, artistic form is another. As Spirit may be communicated through bread and wine so he may be communicated through any material form in a sacramental universe. Anthropologists tell us that religion and art arose as one cultural phenomenon. The inter-relation should remain for the benefit of both. Each represents a penetration of Reality and they work best as they employ each other. A still life by Redon is sacred art, an ill-prepared sermon abuses God. The involvement of art with aesthetics and beauty prevents narrowness in religion. The insistence in religion upon goodness redeems art. People today hunger for spiritual food and new forms can communicate ancient truths. Art seeks always for new forms and ancient truth is the bedrock of religion. What is so old and new as Henry Moore's *Madonna and Child*?

Peter Eugene Ball, Christus, 1990. Wood, copper and gold leaf. Height 152. Winchester Cathedral.

Above Glen Rosa

Thomas A. Clark

LATE ONE AFTERNOON, coming across a stretch of moor above Glen Rosa on the island of Arran, tired after a day of rough walking and having to watch every step among tussocks and hidden rivulets, I happened to look up and see, some yards away, a shape in the fading light. I looked at it and it looked back. There seemed a mutual attraction and incomprehension, a detached curiosity on both sides. The moment stretched out in that stillness when the usual business of assessing or judging or manoeuvering for advantage has broken down or been left behind. It was only when this whole process started up again, when my mind struggled into recognition, that the stag took off down the hillside.

That the animal seemed startled not by a physical movement but by an exertion of thought is part of the point I want to make: categorisation is a cruelty, an attempt at containment from which wild things rightly take flight. But this reflection is secondary in interest to the fact that we can and do, on rare occasions, go beyond such classifications to an unmediated participation in what is happening. If a man and a stag can look at one another, then the moment is beautiful not because of any brightness or keenness that surrounds it, not for any significance it contains or for the consequences that might follow, but because, on the contrary, it seems quite ordinary and matter-of-fact. We feel that this is the way the world should be, that this is the way it is, beyond the deer fence of our own fear and greed.

This is the sort of encounter I like to have with poetry, art or music, the sense of something strange and new which, for all its poise and apparent autonomy, somehow concerns me. Perhaps the sensation is more obvious in the visual arts because of the material, self-sufficient nature of art objects, and because of the distancing effect of vision. The work presents itself as a held presence, an object we can contemplate. It is not immediately obvious that it is there for my gratification. It is not a conundrum to puzzle over, hardly even something to look at. It is simply something to be with. For all we know, it might be a wild creature, a dangerous, possibly violent individual, or it might be entirely nonchalant and disengaged. At any rate, we stand our ground, both myself and the object. For the moment at least no intention or declaration, no admiration or dismissal, comes between us. Each is solid and opaque. I like art which has this element of strangeness. I like art that I do not understand.

This does not mean that a work must necessarily be avant-garde or intimidating in its originality, for the same frisson can occur with entirely traditional and figurative works, only that there must be some quality in it that carries me beyond my expectations, to place me, for a moment at least, before a reality that is prior to all my categories, my antipathies or allegiances. The advantage of work which is experimental or formally innovative is that we are less likely to approach it with so many preconceptions. When a work is situated within a particular genre, we must often wait until our consciousness of its family likeness fades before its individual features start to show through. Art which continues to engage us over a long acquaintance must be strong enough in presence or rich enough in variety to overcome all the assumptions and indifferences of familiarity.

The situation is not very different if we are making art rather than looking at it. The artist works towards a perception, a configuration or harmony that is complete and accomplished and which will satisfy him at a deeper level than the sophisticated, calculating, discursive intellect can reach. Whether it is the result of a single gesture or of many months of loving attention, an artist looks forward to the moment when his work is charged with a life of its own, when he comes up against it as he would a stranger and can see it for the first time. He wants that feeling of authority from his own work which assures him it is real, that it exists outside himself and his intentions. When we look at a piece of our own work and think that it is good, we mean that it possesses this aura of authenticity, that it is more than the sum of the experience, care, passion and thought that we have put into it. The life it leads beyond us allows us to praise it.

To seek out such satisfactions, rather than to make paintings or sculpture, is to be an artist. It requires dedication, energy, lightness, tenacity, intelligence, simplicity and many other qualities, an articulation of a broad range of human abilities. The business of exhibiting and selling, of fashion and reputation, of reception and criticism, is accessory rather than essential to it. The sort of art we make is accessory rather than essential. To be an artist is, by whatever means, to be in pursuit of the miraculous. Or, to use Picasso's more precise distinction, it is not to seek but to find. It is to deliberately go beyond deliberation. Art is not a collection of rare and expensive artefacts, not something that may or may not interest us, not something we take up like stamp-collecting. It is a realm which, at significant moments, we have access to, a meadow in the unfenced region of the spirit.

Whether it is an encounter with a stag, a dazzle on water, a duet for piano and oboe floating in the moonlight, or a sudden clarity in a conversation, there are occasions in which we are completely engaged, in which there is not an intensification or heightening of our everyday consciousness but a break with it. It is as if while on a walk we were to leap across a stream and arrive at a whole new disposition of our faculties. There is balance, awareness, adequacy. On the far side of analysis and speculation, things have a grain and an outline yet are not separate from the ground they inhabit. Nothing is or can be erratic. Everything is granted permission. Perceiver and perceived are parts of a single impulse. If we are receptive to them, such moments may become reservoirs of power, visions or intimations which will change and determine the whole course of our lives. They may become a value which we set above the habitual or secular.

We can make art which is a description of this transcendent state, or in praise of it, or as a means of attaining it. On the other hand, we can make art which is concerned only to be good art but which in accomplishing this aim, in finding itself, leaps beyond its own resources. In all these cases, the art is not secular. It is not content to remain within a known horizon or motive but is charged with a value, an aspiration. A non-secular art cannot, however, be identified by any bench mark. It is a resonance, a struggle, an achievement, not a style nor an ethic. It may obey the rules of a rational system to rise to the level of necessities and laws, or in spontaneous expression carve through layers of the self. It may refer beyond itself or insist on a surface, a texture. We cannot, in the present age, as some artists and critics would have us do, identify the non-secular through signs and symbols, through a political or aesthetic persuasion, or in any particular practice. An art which is apparently mundane in its subject matter and presentation may have a vivacity that is altogether singular, while an ostensibly religious art can be quite superficial, devoid of any religious devotion or awe.

An art which is entirely within prescribed areas of knowledge and feeling is religion, politics, anthropology or decor rather than art. It is only art if it makes the eyes shine. It is only art if it goes beyond its own strengths and weaknesses. Everything else is craft, onanism or accountancy. All the rituals of working, from sharpening pencils, priming canvases, brewing the coffee, to more arcane strategies and practices, are ablutions or preparations for the moment when the work in hand comes to life and moves off into its own territory. It is not art unless it makes demands on both artist and viewer, challenging them, enlarging them. Art is a way of knowledge, a gnosis. Only by travelling that particular path can we arrive at that particular destination.

It is inadequate and unskillful, therefore, to say only that we like or dislike works of art. We should try to experience them. If a work is difficult or remote, we should allow it that distance. We should try to remain for a while in that difficulty and uncertainty. The itch to think and to understand is imperative in human beings and will not be denied for long, but only by way of not understanding can we come to any understanding. What Hegel says of the philosophical mind applies also to our critical approach to works of art, "The tendency of all man's endeavours is to understand the world, to appropriate it and subdue it to himself: and to this end the positive reality of the world must be as it were crushed and pounded, in other words idealised". If we find the world to be now so crushed and pounded that our own chances of survival are threatened, if we discover at last our own liberty and growth to be consanguine with that of things, we must resist the urge to subjection and appropriation. We must be kind enough to leave things to their own space and shape, and art can teach us the joy of such generosity, the pleasure it is when things are unlabelled, singular, self-governed.

One of the first virtues required in looking at art is acceptance. The viewer needs to accept what is presented, to accept it as a gift is accepted. He should not look ungratefully for some other gift. He should not immediately think of its value, as a commodity, as an acquisition, as a contribution to art. The material fact of the work, its internal relations, the presence it holds in a space, must all be readily allowed. We should be quiet enough to let the work's force or delicacy register. We should remain with a work for long enough to let this happen. In the making of art, acceptance is first of all a respect for the material circumstances of a work, then a participation in its evolution, a tolerance of the direction in which it is going. Bad practice consists of making arbitrary demands on intractable materials, in the falsification of appearances, in a formal or stylistic complacency.

Rather than moulding the world to our convenience, I take it that the religious life begins with a reverence for the world (by whatever name it might be called, Reality, God, Mind etc.) and continues through a piety which tempers the individual to an acceptance of the order of things. I don't mean that we accept as final any political or social order. It is a step by step recovery of our lost integrity. Instead of being beside ourselves, carried away in projects, worries, desires, opinions, expectations, gossip or asperities, we are present in and before what is going on. This is what is meant by purity of heart. We are straight in our thoughts and actions, single and uncompounded, living an alert life, free from the distortions of will or personal history. Being contemporary with events, our personal history is cancelled.

In many traditions, we begin with moral and devotional observance and progress through detachment and contemplation to unity of being and rightness of action. Without such a framework, the way is less certain and we may have to rely on nothing more than a sense of direction. "There is only one fault," says Simone Weil, "incapacity to feed on light". We are on the path when we move towards the light, when we recognise a value, when we seek out those experiences which risk the loss of self for the duties and delights of immediacy. When we give up the anxiety of maintaining a form, when we are brave enough to give ourselves without qualification to a sound, a scent, a picture on a wall, then we are on the path.

Although comparatively few artists, in the West at least, now work within a specific religious tradition, many have begun to feel that their work has some sort of spiritual content. What they mean by this is seldom very clearly defined. It may often be no more than an instinctive aversion to the posturing, commercialism and general cynicism of the contemporary art world. More circumspect artists may have the conviction that their work gives information about, or experience of, the spirit, of something larger and deeper than the surface consciousness and its mundane concerns, that it praises or is an act of devotion to a transcendent reality, or that it is itself an adventure of the spirit, taking off into unknown territory. These artists are perhaps less remote than they think from others who do not make such grandiose claims and who apparently live more squarely within an existing situation. The American painter Ad Reinhardt maintained that "There is only one art". If authentic art is an arrival, as I have tried to outline here, then it is something other than a detachable content or programme. A vision of the seriousness of art can lead artists to probe more deeply into art's nature and to question at every stage their own practice and achievements. But there is also the danger that a vision can become myopic and that an intended significance can be merely portentous. In art as in life, we need constantly to separate out and throw away those parts of our activity that are inessential, those ideas and predilections which are unfruitful or debilitating. Like our apprehensions of God, art is not this, not that. Notions of the spiritual in art, like any other such speculations, are only useful if they place us more immediately before or in the midst of the work itself.

Yet there is no doubt that, as art gives evidence of a humanity that remains in potential for most members of the human race, so it is one means to practice and develop that humanity. As small intrusions of reality, perhaps no more than a shape on a bare hillside, can point beyond our attachments and illusions, so works of art can be both self-possessed and exemplary. I am glad that art exists for the same reason I am glad that open country still exists. Both are good in themselves and need no further justification, no evidence of utility to excuse their existence. Surely we have come to feel that a properly exercised humanity requires a margin, a supplement, and is implicated in the condition of all that is not human. Both art and wild landscape are places I can come to. They are places that may confront me with the unexpected, the as yet unnamed. Their varied rewards and hazards draw upon a reservoir of abilities and perspicacities I scarcely know I possess. A new work of art is an occasion, at once an adventure and a homecoming. In meeting the challenge of its gaze, the rift between ourselves and the present is healed. We are forced or persuaded to come out of whatever project or passion has ensnared us, into the world. If the life of an artist consists of clarifying his vision, of bringing himself more and more into tune with the needs of his work, of granting his work its own seriousness and dignity, allowing it to leap and sing, then the life of the spirit is to make oneself transparent, to thin out and disperse those agglutinations of desire and will which come between us and what is happening around us. It is the ability to feel, to register and respond to everything that is the case. It is to distribute oneself as evenly as the late summer light settling over a mountain ridge.

The Journey

SITES

The Bishop's Hostel Chapel dates from 1907 and is designed and decorated by Temple Moore. Built in brick in the decorative style, it has a Lincolnshire decorative five light east window by H Victor Milner.

The nave and chancel are in one and the interior has a pointed wooden tunnel vaulted roof.

The 18th century Bishop's Hostel now serves as Lincoln Theological College.

The Bishop's Palace, Lincoln, is one of the most important medieval domestic buildings in the country and reflects the wealth and power of the medieval Bishops of Lincoln. It was begun by Bishop Chesney in c.1163, continued by Bishop Hugh, 1186–1200, and completed in c.1224 by Hugh Wells. Bishop Burghersh, 1320–40, was given license to repair and crenellate the walls in 1329 and the final major contribution was made by Bishop Alnwick, 1436–49, who built the gate tower and the chapel range and made other alterations.

Samuel Buck, 1696 – 1779, North View of Lincoln Bishop's Palace, 1726. Engraving. 18 x 36. Collection Usher Gallery, Lincoln.

As a result of the violent upheavals of the Reformation, the 16th century saw the slow decline of the medieval palace which was only used occasionally as a residency for the Bishops of Lincoln after the mid-16th century.

The Palace suffered badly during the Lincolnshire Rebellion in 1536, and in 1648, during the Civil War, the Palace was besieged and severely damaged. It fell into decay in the late 17th and 18th centuries and was restored in 1838. The Alnwick Tower was reconstructed in 1876 with an attractive oriel window to the north. The Chapel was almost totally demolished in c.1725. It had a large east window of which no details remain.

In 1954 the ruins of the Palace were taken into the care of the Ministry of Public Building Works. The site is now open to the public and managed by English Heritage.

The Church of St Mary Magdalene with St Paul-in-the-Bail, Lincoln, was built between 1280 and 1299 just outside the Cathedral close, to take parish services out of the western part of the Cathedral. The church never had a graveyard and parishioners were buried in the minster burial ground.

Of the late 13th century building nothing now exists as the church was re-built in 1695 and again by G F Bodley in 1882.

William Gavin Herdman, 1805 – 1882, Exchequergate, Lincoln, 1853 (left – Church of St Mary Magdalene with St Paul-in-the-Bail). Watercolour on paper. 50.8 x 68.6. Collection Usher Gallery, Lincoln.

The interior is lofty with a narrow north aisle and a fine ceiled wagon roof by Bodley, decorated with crosses in the chancel. The organ prospect and screen are also by Bodley.

Temple Bruer was founded in the mid-12th century as an establishment of the Knights Templar, a military religious order that originated at the time of the crusades.

The role of the Templars was to protect the pilgrims and to guard the Shrines of the Holy Land. In order to support their work they established estate-centres or 'Preceptories', such as Temple Bruer, throughout Europe.

Temple Bruer derives the second part of its name from the heathland, the "terra vastata et Brueria" on which it is situated, about 15 miles south of Lincoln. The Templars were among the first colonists of this wilderness and due to the huge sheepwalks on the heath, Temple Bruer was the second wealthiest Preceptory in England by the early 14th century. On the suppression of the Templars in 1312, the estate passed to the Hospitallers, another military order whose function was to provide hospitals and accommodation for weary or poor pilgrims. Templer Bruer was associated with the Hospitallers Commandery at Eagle, near Lincoln, until the dissolution of the Hospitallers in 1540-1.

The 12th century 'Round Church' of the Templars, designed to imitate the Church of the Holy Sepulchre, Jerusalem, survived until the 18th century but the Church gradually became a ruin.

The only surviving feature above ground today is the 13th century south east tower. The tower was restored in 1961 and is now a Scheduled Ancient Monument in the guardianship of Lincolnshire County Council.

Frederick Mackenzie, 1787 – 1854, Stow Church. Watercolour on paper. 77 x 102. Collection Usher Gallery, Lincoln.

The Church of St Mary, Stow-in-Lindsey, is one of the most monumental Anglo-Saxon churches in England, dominating the remote village of Stow, about 10 miles north of Lincoln.

The Anglo-Saxon name 'Stow' means 'a holy place' and attempts have been made to connect the Church with the Cathedral of the see of Lindsey, founded at the Roman site of Sidnacester in 678.

It is more likely that the Church was founded by Bishop Aelfnoth of Dorchester c975, to serve as Head Minster or 'mother church' of the Lincolnshire part of his diocese.

The Church today is of 'cruciform' or cross-shaped plan with a central tower, aisleless nave and chancel and a north and south transept.

The Anglo-Saxon remains consist of the central crossing with its four massive arches and the north and south transepts. The Church was rebuilt in the early 11th century by Bishop Eadnoth and endowed by Earl Leofric and Lady Godiva in c1054.

The nave and elaborate chancel are of Norman date and the nave was probably built by Remigius, first Norman Bishop of Lincoln, sometime after 1071. Remigius refounded the church as a Benedictine Abbey in 1091, bringing monks from Eynsham in Oxfordshire, but his successor, Bishop Bloet, removed the monks and annexed the church to his Lincoln see in c1094-5.

The present octagonal font dates from the 13th century and is decorated on each side with a carved motif, including a pentangle and a green man, none of them Christian.

The Saxon tower was replaced in the 15th century and the church was extensively restored in the 1850s by the architect, John Loughborough Pearson.

The Rest, Priorygate/Eastgate, Lincoln is a low, picturesque, half-timbered building, late 19th century in its present appearance but the brick east gable dates from the 17th century.

Originally a private dwelling house, from the mid 18th century the property was in the occupation of the Lievesley family who were bakers.

In 1898 the lease was assigned to the local industrialist, Alfred Shuttleworth, who undertook to repair the building and to provide "a shelter for persons waiting in all weathers for the carriers' carts on market and other days". (Chapter Act 19.3.1898).

Shuttleworth's acquisition and improvement of the Rest were part of his scheme for enhancing all the property facing his house in Eastgate.

In 1912 the Dean and Chapter resolved to extend his tenancy of the house and shelter on a yearly basis on the terms of the repairing lease.

The Rest remained open as a public shelter until the property was renovated for occupation by the Cathedral Fabric Fund Office in 1987.

Thomas Girtin, 1775 – 1802, Lincoln Cathedral, 1795. Watercolour on paper. 38 x 28. Collection Usher Gallery, Lincoln.

The Cathedral Church of St Mary, Lincoln was founded in 1072 when the Council of Windsor decreed that the headquarters of Bishops should be in fortified towns rather than villages and Remigius, Bishop of Dorchester, moved his see to Lincoln.

Since 1072 the original structure has undergone many changes, and the Cathedral is essentially of three periods: Norman, Early English and 14th–15th century.

The first Cathedral was consecrated in 1092. It was a cruciform building with the east end having a main apse with smaller apses to the chancel aisles. This church was damaged by fire in 1141 and the original elevation of the Norman west front was considerably altered under Bishop Alexander, 1123–1148, who replaced the three portals and added elaborate figured and geometric ornament, and the frieze of sculptured scenes from the Old and New Testament.

In 1185, the Cathedral was destroyed by an earthquake and in 1192 St Hugh of Avalon, Bishop of Lincoln 1186–1200, began a major rebuilding programme. St Hugh began rebuilding from the east and by 1240 the remaining west front and towers were incorporated into the Early English design.

In 1256 the East End of St Hugh's Cathedral was extended in order to accommodate a more fitting shrine to the local saint. The result is the beautifully proportioned memorial Retrochoir, the 'Angel Choir', completed in 1280.

The 'nave' of the Angel Choir receives its light from the early eight light *East Window* (c.1275).

The window of the North Transept, *The Dean's Eye,* of c.1210 is a fine example of plate tracery and 13th century glass whose principal subject is the Last Judgment. The corresponding window in the South Transept, *The Bishop's Eye,* dates from c.1320 and is filled with flowing tracery and fragments of medieval glass inserted in 1788.

In c.1311 the central tower of the Cathedral was raised and completed with a lead-covered timber spire. The western towers were completed in the 15th century and the Cathedral reached its full external magnificence. This was retained until 1549 when the great central spire was blown down in a storm. The spires on the Western Towers became unsafe by the late 18th century and were dismantled in 1807.

Since the 18th century much strengthening of the fabric has been undertaken and an extensive programme of restoration commenced in the 1960's.

During recent years the Dean and Chapter have commissioned several major pieces of contemporary craft for the Cathedral.

The Treasury, which was established in 1960 to house the fine silver plate from Diocesan churches and personal plate of the Cathedral's Bishops, has contemporary stained glass by Geoffrey Clarke.

In 1984, the potter Robin Welch, was commissioned to make five great candle holders and pots in memory of Gilbert of Sempringham, the 12th century saint, and the Order he founded in South Lincolnshire. Technically they are at the limit of what is possible on a potter's wheel.

In 1986, the Chapter commissioned a striking contemporary sculpture to celebrate the 800th Anniversary of St Hugh. Designed by the then Lincolnshire based jewellery designer, David Poston and built by the Gloucestershire based blacksmith, Alan Evans, the sculpture stands over the Head Shrine of St Hugh.

"I have always held and am prepared against all evidence to maintain that the Cathedral of Lincoln is out and out the most precious piece of architecture in the British Isles and roughly speaking worth any two other cathedrals we have." *John Ruskin 1819–1900*

Tupholme Abbey was founded in the mid-12th century by Premonstratensian (or Norbertine) canons from Newhouse, on the south bank of the Humber. Tupholme lies about 10 miles east of Lincoln in an unusual concentration of medieval religious houses lining the Witham Valley below the city. In 1536, at its dissolution, there were nine canons but at its height the abbey housed at least 24.

Quarried for building stone since the dissolution, few of the other monastic remains can rival Tupholme, where the south wall of the refectory still stands, incorporating a unique stone pulpit.

Tupholme has experienced many changes. Once an abbey, it became in turn a stately home, a picturesque ruin, a farm and eventually a group of farm labourers' cottages. The cottages fell empty and in the 1970s part of the abbey precinct was ploughed up. About three years ago the derelict cottages were demolished. The future looked bleak.

Heritage Lincolnshire bought the site in December 1988 and together with The Friends of Tupholme Abbey set about the task of transformation. At Easter 1990 the site was declared open to the public. The refectory wall is being repaired and with sensitive management the 20 acres of grassland around the abbey ruins will once again support the variety of wildlife so rarely seen on modern pastures.

The Journey

BIOGRAPHICAL
INFORMATION

Roger Ackling was born in Isleworth, London, in 1947. He now lives and works in London.

Recent exhibitions include the Museum of Arles, in the Cloisters of Saint Trophine, 1988; Concept Space, Shibukawa and White Art, Tokyo, Japan; P.P.O.W., New York, and the Graeme Murray Gallery, Edinburgh, 1989; Vaughan and Vaughan, Minneapolis and the well received exhibition 'Works from Norfolk' at Annely Juda, Fine Art, London, 1990. His work is represented in public collections internationally including the Tate Gallery, the Arts Council of Great Britain, British Council, Kunstmuseum, Zurich, Musee Reatto, Arles and the Hiroshima Museum of Modern Art.

Craigie Aitchison was born in Scotland in 1926, and now lives and works in London. He has had many one person exhibitions including Kettles Yard, Cambridge, 1979, a major Arts Council retrospective at the Serpentine, London in 1981 and most recently at the Albemarle Gallery, London. He has featured in most of the exhibitions concerning art and the spirit, notably 'Prophecy and Vision' at Arnolfini, 1982, 'The Glass of Vision', Chichester Cathedral, 1987 and in 1989, 'A Spiritual Dimension' and 'New Icons'. His work is represented in many public collections including the Arts Council of Great Britain, Contemporary Art Society, Tate Gallery, Newcastle Region Art Gallery, New South Wales, Australia and the Scottish National Gallery of Modern Art, Edinburgh. He was elected a Royal Academician in 1989.

Wendy Beckett is a contemplative nun who lives in the grounds of an enclosed monastery in East Anglia. She has contributed to many magazines including Modern Painters, Artscribe and Art Monthly, and writes regularly for Catholic newspapers in England. In 1988 her book 'Contemporary Women Artists' was published by Phaidon.

Thomas A Clark was born in Greenock, Scotland, and now lives in Gloucestershire. He is a poet whose work is primarily concerned with the landscape as a place of simultaneous self-discovery and otherness. With his wife Laurie, he runs Cairn Gallery, in Nailsworth, Gloucestershire, which has a particular interest in the relations between art and landscape.

Stephen Cox was born in Bristol in 1946 and currently lives and works in London. Since his one-man exhibition at the Lisson Gallery, London in 1976 he has had numerous one-man shows in England and abroad including the Galleria La Salita, Rome, 1982, Nigel Greenwood Gallery, London, 1983, 1984, Arnolfini, Bristol, and Museum of Modern Art, Oxford, 1985, Sixth Indian Triennale, New Delhi, and Tate Gallery, 1986, Artsite, Bath, 1988 and Galleria Carini, Florence, 1987 and 1989. Notable group exhibitions include British Sculpture in the 20th century, Whitechapel Art Gallery, London, 1981, Aperto '82', Venice Biennale, 1982, The Sculpture Show, Hayward Gallery, London, and New Art, Tate Gallery, London, 1983, An International Survey of Recent Painting and Sculpture, Museum of Modern Art, New York, 5 Scultori Inglesi, Artra Studio, Milan, 1984, The British Show, Art Gallery of Western Australia, Perth and tour, 1985, Forty Years of Modern Art, Tate Gallery, London, 1986, 'Freedom to Touch', Laing Art Gallery, Newcastle and tour, 1986 – 1987, 40 Years of British Sculpture, Ahkanator Gallery, Cairo, 1987, 'The Tree of Life', Royal Festival Hall, London and tour, 1989 – 1990 and 'New Icons', Mead Gallery, University of Warwick and tour, 1990.

His work is represented in a number of public collections including the Arts Council of Great Britain and the Tate Gallery and recent commissions include 'Song', a sculpture for the new Cairo Opera House and 'Ganapati and Devi' at Broadgate, London.

Don Cupitt is lecturer in the Philosophy of Religion at the University of Cambridge and Dean of Emmanuel College, Cambridge. He has recently completed a major series of books concerning faith in the post modern age; Life Lines published 1986, The Long Legged Fly, 1987, The New Christian Ethics, 1988, and Radicals and the Future of the Church, 1989.

Richard Devereux was born in Lincoln in 1956, where he continues to live and work. Selected one-person shows include 'Circles', Usher Gallery, Lincoln 1984, 'Assembled Rites' Artsite, Bath 1987, 'On Sacred Ground' Cairn Gallery, Gloucestershire and 'Beyond the Hall of Dreams', New Art Centre London, 1989. His work has featured in 20th century British Sculpture, Roche Court, Wiltshire, 1988, 1989, 1990 and at the Salisbury Festival, 1988 and is represented in many public collections, including Lincolnshire and Humberside Arts, Tate Gallery, Bodleian Library, Oxford and the University Library, Cambridge.

Jennifer Durrant was born in Brighton in 1942 and now lives and works in London. She has had many one person exhibitions including Arnolfini, Bristol, 1979, Museum of Modern Art, Oxford, 1980, Nicola Jacobs Gallery, 1982, 1985, Serpentine Gallery, London, 1987, and Newlyn Orion, Penzance, 1988.

Since 1976 her work has featured in many important exhibitions, notably 'British Painting 1952 – 77', Royal Academy, London 1977; 'The New Context in Europe', Studio Marconi, Milan, 1980; 'Artists in National Parks', Victoria & Albert Museum, London, touring 1988 – 89; 'The Presence of Painting : Aspects of British Abstraction', 1958 – 88, Mappin Art Gallery, Sheffield, touring 1988 – 89; 'The Experience of Painting', Laing Art Gallery, Newcastle touring 1989, 'Images of Paradise', Survival International, Harewood House, Leeds 1989 and 'Now for the Future', purchases for the Arts Council Collection 1984 –, Hayward Gallery, London, 1990.

Her work is represented in numerous public collections including the Arts Council of Great Britain, British Council, Contemporary Art Society, Tate Gallery and Museum of Fine Arts, Boston, Mass. In 1988 she was awarded the Athena Art Award.

Garry Fabian Miller was born in Bristol in 1957. Between 1980-88 he lived and worked at Lowfield Farm, Lincolnshire, and now lives on Dartmoor. He has had many one person exhibitions including Arnolfini, Bristol, Axiom, Cheltenham and the Natural History Museum, London. In 1987 he completed a commission and exhibition, 'The Tree a Return to Grace', for the Usher Gallery, Lincoln. During the late 1980's Fabian Miller made work for environmental landscape exhibitions such as 'Tree of Life', Arts Council touring exhibition, and 'Artists in National Parks' at the Victoria and Albert Museum. His work is in many public collections including the Bibliothèque Nationale, Paris, Victoria and Albert Museum, the Government Art Collection, and the National Museum of Film, Photography and Television Bradford. He is currently preparing work for a one-person exhibition at Newlyn in the autumn, 1990.

Jon Groom was born in Powys, Wales in 1953. He now lives and works in New York. He has exhibited for a number of years with the Nicola Jacobs Gallery, London, and has had one person shows at the Ruther Siegel Gallery, New York, 1985, Galerie Wasserman and Edition E, Munich, 1987, and Lorenzelli Arte, Milan in 1988.

He was also represented in the exhibition "The Presence of Painting: Aspects of British Abstraction 1958–88", Mappin Gallery, Sheffield and tour. His work is in the collections of the Arts Council, Victoria and Albert Museum, The Chase Manhatten Bank, London, Städtische Galerie Ingolstadt and the Kunsthalle Mannheim.

Sue Hilder was born in Northumberland in 1964 and is presently studying for an MA at Humberside College, Hull.

Her work has been featured in a number of group shows, including 'New Art in Yorkshire', City Art Gallery and Jacob Cramer College Gallery, Leeds, 1987, 'Testing the Means', Third Northlands Art Show, Cheltenham and Gloucester City Art Gallery, 1988, 'On Show', Usher Gallery, Lincoln, 1988 and 'Germinations 5' (one of ten artists to represent the UK in touring exhibition of European graduates), Lyon, Bonn, Breda and Glasgow, 1989-1990.

Eileen Lawrence was born in Leith, Scotland in 1946, where she continues to live and work. Principal one person exhibitions include Arnolfini, Bristol, 1978, Fischer Fine Art, London, 1980, 1985 and Artsite, Bath, 1986. Her work is represented in many public collections including the Tate Gallery, the British Council, Contemporary Arts Society and the National Gallery of Modern Art, Canberra, Australia. Her work featured in 'Scottish Art since 1900', Barbican Art Gallery, London and in 'New North' at the Tate Gallery, Liverpool, 1990.

Richard Long was born in Bristol in 1945, where he still lives. One of Britain's leading artists, in 1989 he was awarded the Turner Prize, Tate Gallery – Patrons of New Art.

Since his first one person show in Dusseldorf in 1968, he has exhibited extensively throughout the world and is to have a one-person show at the Tate Gallery this autumn.

In addition to numerous publications by the artist, a major monograph was published by

Thames & Hudson in 1986 to co-incide with an exhibition at the Guggenheim Museum, New York.

A film 'Stones and Flies', Richard Long in the Sahara, was recently produced by the Arts Council in association with Channel 4 Television.

Rupert Martin was born in 1957. He was Exhibition Organiser at the Photographer's Gallery, London 1980-83, and Gallery Co-ordinator at the Arnolfini, Bristol 1984-87. Exhibitions and projects he has arranged include Stephen Cox, Sculpture 1977-85, Karel Appel, Paintings 1980-87 and the Forest of Dean Sculpture Project.

As a freelance Arts Consultant, (Art Landmarks), 1987–89, he curated Sidney Nolan – A Retrospective and the exhibition, New Icons: Christian Iconography in Contemporary Art. In 1989 he began studying for ordination at Trinity College, Bristol.

His book on the Forest of Dean Project, The Sculpted Forest, was published by Redcliffe Press, Bristol, in 1990.

Leonard McComb was born in Glasgow in 1930, and now works and lives in London. Since the 1976 Arts Council exhibition 'Human Clay', his work has featured in many important exhibitions, notably the 'British Art Show', 1979, 1985, the 1980 Venice Biennale, 'British Sculpture in the 20th Century', Whitechapel Art Gallery, 1981, 'Hard Won Image', Tate Gallery, 1984, 'Representation Abroad', Hirshhorn Museum, Washington DC, 1986, 'Art of Watercolour', Norwich Castle Museum, and 'Artists Self Portraits', Artsite, Bath, 1987.

His work was the subject of a major touring exhibition organised by the Arts Council and the Museum of Modern Art, Oxford in 1983 and more recently he has had two successful exhibitions of painting of Provence at the Gillian Jason Gallery, London. He was elected an Associate Member of the Royal Academy in 1987.

Malcolm Miles is Director of the British Health Care Arts Centre, which is the national organisation for advice, publication, research and development of art in the National Health Service. He is an adviser to the Department of Health and Scottish Office on art in hospitals, and to the Arts Council Steering Group on the Percent for Art. Before taking up his present post, he was Deputy Head of Fine Art at the Kent Institute of Art and Design, where he developed new course elements between the Schools of Fine Art and Architecture. He has also undertaken 4 visits to Romania and Bulgaria for the British Council, through the Cultural Exchange, and makes regular research visits to the USA. In the summer of 1990, he will be a visiting Fellow to the School of Architecture of Curtin University of Technology, Perth, Western Australia.

He is a painter, with works in public and private collections in Britain and the USA, and a writer on art and environment for magazines such as Resurgence, Art Monthly, New Art Examiner, Landscape Design, and Artists Newsletter. His book, Art for Public Places – critical essays – was published in 1989 by Winchester School of Art Press.

Glen Onwin was born in Scotland in 1947 and lives and works in Edinburgh. One person exhibitions include 'The Recovery of Dissolved Substances', 1978, at the ICA, London, 'A Mineral Response to Nature', Air Gallery, London, 1982, 'Earth Icons, The Chymical Garden', Artsite, Bath, 1988, and a major exhibition 'Revenges of Nature', the Fruitmarket Gallery, Edinburgh and Third Eye Centre, Glasgow, 1988-89, accompanied by an extensive publication. His work featured in 'Scottish Art Since 1900' at the Barbican Art Gallery, London, 1990.

Keir Smith was born in Kent in 1950 and now lives and works in London. In 1979 he was appointed Sculptor in Residence at Grizedale Forest, Cumbria, where his work can still be seen. Public sited commissions include 'Dendron' for Yorkshire Sculpture Park, 1983, 'The Iron Road', for the Forestry Commission, Forest of Dean Sculpture Trail, 1986 and 'Windborn' for the National Garden Festival in Stoke on Trent, 1986.

He has had many one person exhibitions including 'Sailing Ancient Seas', Ceolfrith Gallery, Sunderland and Ikon Gallery, Birmingham, 1982, 'The Coniston Variations' Richard Demarco, Edinburgh, 1983, 'Navigator', Rochdale Art Gallery, touring 1984 – 5, 'The Dust of Learning', Artsite, Bath, 1986 and 'The Dreaming Track', Laing Art Gallery, Newcastle and Wolverhampton Art Gallery, 1989.

Since 1973 his work has featured in numerous group shows including 'Art and the Sea', Southampton and ICA, London, 1981, 'Tongue and Groove', Coracle Press Gallery and tour, 1983, 'Sculptors and Modellers', Tate Gallery, 1983, 'A Sense of Place', Ceolfrith Gallery and tour, 1984, 'Small Works' and 'The Eighties', Juda Rowan Gallery, London, 1985, 'Feeling Through Form', Barbican Art Gallery, London, 1986, 'Open Air Sculpture Show', Lincoln and tour, 1986, 'Revelation for the Hands', Leeds City Art Gallery, 1987, 'Artists in National Parks', Victoria & Albert Museum and tour, 1988, 'The Cutting Edge', Manchester City Art Gallery, 1989 and 'Painters and Poets in Print', Artists Books 1970 – 1990, South Bank Centre and tour, 1990.

His work is represented in a number of public collections including the British Council, Northern Art and the Mead Art Gallery, Warwick.

Peter Randall-Page was born in Essex in 1954, and now works and lives in Devon. He has undertaken many public commissions for urban sites and two important landscape projects, a group of wayside shrines for the New Milestones project in Dorset, and the Forest of Dean Sculpture Trail. He is included in many public collections including the Henry Moore Centre for the Study of Sculpture, Leeds City Art Gallery, Usher Gallery, Lincoln, the British Council and the Contemporary Arts Society. Recent exhibitions include the International Garden Festival, Liverpool, 1984, Anne Berthoud Gallery, London, 1985, 'Stoneworks', Powys Castle, Wales, 1988, 'The Cutting Edge', Manchester City Art Gallery and 'Out of the Wood', Crafts Council and Tour, 1989.

The Rev. Canon A K Walker MA, BSc, PhD, is Canon Librarian at Winchester

Cathedral. His PhD thesis on the eighteenth century Anglican theologian and mystic, William Law, was published in 1974. He has taught theology at Wells and Chichester Theological Colleges and has a lifelong interest in the relation between art and religion.

He served with Dean Walter Hussey at Chichester Cathedral as a member of the Dean and Chapter and his commissions for the church include works by Cecil Collins, Patrick Reyntiens and Elizabeth Frink.